Equality for women is an oxymoron
(How to become an equalist)

James Judd

Illustrations by
A. J. Dickens

Equality for women is an oxymoron
(How to become an equalist)

Dedicated to my lovely wife
who incidentally has never once
asked me to put the toilet seat down.

James Judd

Contents

                                              Page

		Page
	Preface	1
1	Equality for women is an oxymoron	5
2	What is an equalist?	11
3	Are men discriminated against?	15
4	Toilet seat syndrome	33
5	Man flu	39
6	Gender discrimination in the law	45
7	The law is an ass	55
8	What part of "No!", do you not understand?	71
9	Rape	85
10	False rape claims	105
11	Domestic violence	123
12	Erin Pizzey	143
13	The Suffragettes	155
14	Women control the means of reproduction	185
15	Cuckoo kids	193
16	Why should I pay for your dog?	205
17	Women should not expect equal pay	217
18	The self-inflicted glass ceiling	239
19	Is the best man for the job a woman?	247
20	Thinking outside the box	255
	Appendix - Helplines and useful contacts	287

Preface

EQUALITY FOR WOMEN IS AN OXYMORON

Preface

"Awfully good" and "fantastically awful" are oxymorons but they have only been oxymorons since "awfully" changed it's meaning from it's original meaning of very good, as in aw-full meaning full-of-awe and was used in the way we now use awe-some or awe-inspiring to it's current meaning of very bad.

I am telling you this because for the purist an oxymoron must have apparently contradictory terms that appear in conjunction such as "awfully good" but in a living language, meanings change and now an oxymoron is used to describe almost any contradiction in terms.

I have no wish to argue semantics so if as a purist you wish take issue with my use of the word oxymoron then please feel free to read "contradiction" in it's place.

I know this book will probably get bad reviews because in it I often put forward an alternative to the distorted version of discrimination we have been force-fed by some of the more extreme feminists for so many years!

Being written from an anti-feminist perspective this book will certainly anger many and may be destined to become the book most thrown at the wall but before you throw it, please try to look at the arguments with an open mind and from both sides.

EQUALITY FOR WOMEN IS AN OXYMORON

I am asking you, if only for the duration of this book to abandon your feminism or your masculinism and join me as an 'equalist' with the objective of equality for all. If after you have done that you still want to throw this book against the wall, then throw it with my blessing!

Chapter 1

Equality for women is an oxymoron!

EQUALITY FOR WOMEN IS AN OXYMORON

Equality for women is an oxymoron!

"Feminism is the idea that we can make both sexes equal by focusing solely on the issues of one of them."

TJ KINCAID

The statement *"Equality for women is an oxymoron"* is bound to raise the hackles of the feminists and I admit this statement was intended to shock but I stand by it.

It's not that I have deliberately set out to provoke, nor is it my intention to make you angry. It's my intention to make you think and to question some of the reasoning used when addressing gender bias in all its forms and to that end I sometimes play Devil's Advocate.

The statement *"Equality for women is an oxymoron"* however is not an example of my playing Devil's Advocate, it's actually true. If you think about it you cannot have equality on only one side.

You either have equality or you do not!

It makes no more sense to make one sex more equal, than to say one animal is more equal.

What most people mean by equality for women is the redressing of the many inequalities suffered by women through history and in many cases still exist today. A just cause but the words "Equality for women" are contradictory.

To have a minister for women who is also the minister for equality means she (and it's always been a woman so far) must be both impartial and partisan at the same time (now that's what I call multi-tasking!). Her very role is inequitable, how can it be equal to have a minister for women and yet no minister for men?

At a stretch it could be argued that if women are the only ones disadvantaged by discrimination then women will always be the beneficiaries of more equality, therefore equality is always for the benefit of women but this is not so and men suffer as much from discrimination as women, making equality for women both oxymoronic and discriminatory in itself.

The false premise that equality is only for the benefit of women was demonstrated when Phillip Davies proposed that there should be a debate on some of the issues that predominantly effect men on International Men's Day (yes there is an International Men's Day). His proposal was refused and the very idea laughed at by feminist MP Jess Phillips.

Source:
https://www.youtube.com/watch?v=8XX6ATwQv7Q&feature=youtu.be&a

Feminism and misogyny are two sides of the same coin and

are equally toxic.

The only difference I can see between the feminist and the misogynist is that the feminists proudly proclaim their discrimination while even the word misogynist is only ever used as an insult.

The first step in solving any problem is to correctly identify it. With gender discrimination we are being held back because in many cases we haven't yet taken this first step.

The feminists would have us choose either to side with women or to side with men. You are with us or you are against us. This is a mistake! We must choose equality for all or discrimination for all. You are for equality or you are against equality.

Too often we see people making demands for equality while advocating gender discrimination.

If you truly seek equality you cannot be partisan, you must oppose inequality wherever it is found regardless of who may gain or loose from its elimination.

Equalism is self-leveling. If one gender is disproportionally disadvantaged they will automatically be disproportionally advantaged by the progress towards true equality.

EQUALITY FOR WOMEN IS AN OXYMORON

Chapter 2

What is an equalist?

EQUALITY FOR WOMEN IS AN OXYMORON

What is an equalist?

> *Equality:*
> *"The state or quality of being equal; correspondence in quantity, degree, value, rank or ability."*
>
> DICTIONARY DEFINITION

An equalist is someone who stands in the middle ground between the two extremes of feminism and misogyny. Someone who wants equality and is therefore necessarily gender blind.

I want equality and to that end I call myself an 'Equalist'. I am therefore against the pseudo equality advocated by feminism where only things that are deemed to disadvantage women are considered and only one side of the argument looked at. Such a one-sided approach to equality makes true equality quite impossible.

Gender discrimination that disadvantages one gender or both exists but if you try to remedy discrimination on one side by counter balancing it with discrimination on the other, you will simply be adding another layer of discrimination.

The reason feminists present a one-sided account is to make as strong a case as possible for giving women a better deal but the unintended consequence of this is that where women are disadvantaged the feminists are often misattributing the blame and so in their fight for equality they are often aiming at the wrong target and their insistence that men are the root of all evil often means that the real problem is never addressed.

With the rise of feminism both men and women have been conditioned to see women as victims who must be given special treatment to help them overcome the 'disability' of being born female, but being a woman is not a disability and it is insulting and demeaning to women to treat them as if it were.

Men and women are equal, different but equal.

All that is needed for women to throw off the yoke of domestic servitude is for someone to look-after the kids but be careful what you wish for, swapping the shackles of the kitchen sink for the shackles of the production line or the office desk may not be all it's cracked up to be.

If women are always the losers in gender discrimination then women will always be the winners when discrimination is addressed but are women always the losers?

Chapter 3

Are men never discriminated against?

EQUALITY FOR WOMEN IS AN OXYMORON

Are men never discriminated against?

> *"I am dubious about the need for an international men's day in and of itself. For me it is up there with needing a white history month, or able body action day. Men are celebrated, elevated and awarded every day of the week on every day of the year. Being a man is it's own reward. You hit the jackpot when you are born a boy child."*
>
> JESS PHILIPS

Source:
http://www.independent.co.uk/voices/we-need-international-mens-day-about-as-much-as-a-white-history-month-or-able-body-action-day-a6740646.html

In this chapter I will highlight some of the disadvantages of being born a boy child to balance the well-publicised disadvantages of being born a girl child.

The feminists would have us believe that being a man means having more money, more choices and freedom from the fear of attack but the reality is not as one sided as it may seem.

If we take a feminist one-sided view of gender bias then women are clearly discriminated against. We just need to look at domestic violence, the wage gap or the lack of representation in political office and the boardroom but if we do the same thing for men and cherry-pick some of the negative aspects of gender bias from a male perspective then men are also clearly discriminated against so in the interest of balance here is a feminist style, one-sided view of discrimination but this time using men as the victim.

HISTORICALLY MEN ARE EXPENDABLE

If we go back a hundred years, the Suffragettes were fighting for the vote but a hundred years ago the men were fighting for their country, half starved in the lousy disease and rat infested trenches of the First World War, rotting from the feet up while being bayoneted, bombed, shot at and gassed, or if the post traumatic stress all got too much then they were taken out at dawn and shot for cowardice by their own side and almost half the men in the trenches of the First World War did not have the vote either.

The fact is, the vote was restricted to men who had property and was much more about elitism than gender bias.

If we move on to the Second World War, men still had it bad. The average life expectancy of a Spitfire pilot was just 4 weeks and the average life span of a Tail Gunner was even worse at only 3 operations.

Source:
http://www.thetimes.co.uk/tto/archive/battle-of-britain/article2637300.ece
http://www.bbc.co.uk/history/ww2peopleswar/user/02/u2129702.shtml

The average age of an RAF pilot in 1940 was 20 years but some were as young as 18 so even after the Representation of the People Act of 1918 many of the Battle of Britain pilots still did not have the vote.

In the present day wars in Iraq and Afghanistan we still see that almost all the dead are men!

As of 24 July 2015 there were 404 UK fatalities classed as, 'killed as a result of hostile action' only three of whom were female, which is less than 1% even though women make up around 10% of the armed forces.

Source:
https://en.wikipedia.org/wiki/British_Forces_casualties_in_Afghanistan_since_2001
http://www.theguardian.com/uk-news/2015/dec/20/uk-military-could-allow-women-in-close-combat-roles-by-end-of-2016

MEN ARE THE VICTIMS IN MOST VIOLENCE

It's not just in wars that men are dying. Men are much more likely to be the victim of murder or violent crime.

The majority of murder victims are not defenceless old women but young men. The office for national statistics states that…

"In 2011/12, as in previous years, more than two-thirds of homicide victims (68%) were male."

Source:
www.ons.gov.uk/ons/dcp171778_298904.pdf

http://webarchive.nationalarchives.gov.uk/20160105160709/http://www.ons.gov.uk/ons/dcp171776_394478.pdf

Men are also more than three times as likely to die by their own hand, (78%) with 4,858 male suicides and 1,375 female suicides in 2013. Suicide is the leading cause of death of men under 45.

Source:
http://webarchive.nationalarchives.gov.uk/20160105160709/http://www.ons.gov.uk/ons/dcp171778_395145.pdf

A MAN'S LIFE IS WORTH LESS THAN THAT OF A WOMAN

The 'Birkenhead drill' is when women and children are given priority in life threatening situations.

The Birkenhead drill gets it's name from the 1852 sinking of the HMS Birkenhead which sank with a full complement of Her Majesty's Royal Marines on board, all standing to attention on the decks of the doomed ship, waiting stoically to drown in place, while the few lifeboats aboard took the women and children to safety.

It's the Birkenhead drill that is referred to in the line... *"So they stood an' was still to the Birken'ead drill, soldier an' sailor too"*! From the poem, Soldier an' Sailor Too by Rudyard Kipling.

The most frequently quoted example of the Birkenhead drill is when the Titanic went down. There were not enough lifeboats so the captain famously ordered that women and children must go first. The result was that most of the women survived and most of the men did not.

If you are still not convinced that a woman's life is of more importance, then listen to the news reports. The reporter will often give the number of casualties in an accident or terror attack then add the words *"including women and children."*

MOST HIGH RISK JOBS ARE DONE BY MEN

We all know about the equal payday (November 10th in 2017) when women would stop earning if they earned at the same rate as men but how many know about equal death at work day?

The last date I saw for 'Fatal Injuries at Work Day' was January 10th. Less than one third of the way through the first month!!

Source:
http://www.inside-man.co.uk/2015/03/03/97-employees-die-work-men-2009-2014-figures

WOMEN SPEND MORE THAN MEN

Men do earn more than women (at some ages) but women spend more. Who has the best of the deal the one who is earning the money or the one who gets to spend it?

Fathers earn more per hour than equivalent men without

children, this is because men with children NEED to earn more money to provide for their family.

Source:
http://metro.co.uk/2016/04/25/men-with-children-earn-more-than-those-without-5838317/

WOMEN EARN MORE THAN MEN (SOMETIMES)

If you remove the childcare affect from women's earnings then the wage gap is actually reversed with women earning more than men.

The Office for National Statistics divides the statistics for the male/female wage gap into 4 parts by the earner's age. The report shows that between the age of 22 and 29 women earn more than men.

Women who work part time earn more than men who work part time.

Women who do not take a career break also earn more than men.

Source:
https://www.theguardian.com/money/2015/aug/29/women-in-20s-earn-more-men-same-age-study-finds

WOMEN GET THE HOUSE

The old joke says… *"In a divorce the woman gets the house*

and the man gets the mortgage" but this is much too close to the truth to be funny.

There are rarely any winners in a divorce but in 90% of cases, women get the children, the house and an income while men lose all of the above.

Source:
https://www.co-oplegalservices.co.uk/media-centre/articles-jan-apr-2017/divorce-with-kids-who-gets-the-house/

WOMEN PAY MUCH LESS INTO THE PENSION POT BUT TAKE MUCH MORE OUT

When calculating the wage gap no account is taken of the pensions gap.

A working woman who is old enough to get a pension but still below the pension age for a man will be paid both her wages and her pension but only her wages will be counted as earnings so the statistics will show her being paid the same as the man working next to her in the same job but her bank account will be thousands of pounds fuller.

According to The Independent newspaper, the extra pension payments that women get are worth £36,000. Ironically there is a campaign group that calls itself *"Women Against State Pension Inequality"* that is arguing against the equalising of the pension age and threatening a very expensive class action on the grounds of *"fairness and justice"*.

EQUALITY FOR WOMEN IS AN OXYMORON

A Google search for 'Men Against State Pension Inequality' just came up with the 'Women's Fight Against The Pension Changes.'

I wonder if women would still be paid less per hour if this £36,000 were averaged out over a woman's working life (making appropriate adjustment for the fact that women do far fewer hours of paid work).

Source:
http://www.independent.co.uk/money/government-faces-legal-action-over-women-whove-lost-out-on-pensions-a6724191.html

In the 1960s women burned their bras for equality maybe it's time men started wearing them for pension equality.

If you are a man over the age of 65 (at the time of writing) then you have been shortchanged over your pension, so ask yourself this…

For £36,000 and the satisfaction of knowing you have struck a blow for equality would you be prepared to wear a bra for two years?

In the UK, if you live as a woman for two years and are diagnosed with gender dysphoria (which is simply defined as discomfort with your birth gender) then you can apply to be reclassified as a woman.

The only question is whether a man over the age of 65 can claim his 5 years pension back pay retrospectively.

Source:
https://www.gov.uk/apply-gender-recognition-certificate/overview

MEN PAY MORE

FACT:

There is a flood of money going…

    From men to women;

    From men to children;

    From men to the taxman.

The extra money men pay out, dwarfs the effect of women's lower pay rate. This fact is seldom mentioned in the debates over equal pay.

From *"Can I buy you a drink"* on the very first date to the final divorce settlement, it's men doing the paying.

Men are the main breadwinners in two thirds of households, sharing their earnings with their wives and children.

Source:
http://www.theguardian.com/lifeandstyle/2015/oct/20/working-mothers-britain-breadwinner-statistics-income

Men do over 60% of the paid work and are three times more likely to work more than 45 hours a week. If you want men to continue to pay more they must also earn more.

Source:
http://www.telegraph.co.uk/men/relationships/fatherhood/11122773/Society-still-doesnt-like-the-idea-of-stay-at-home-dads.html

MEN ARE DISCRIMINATED AGAINST IN THE CRIMINAL JUSTICE SYSTEM

FACT:

Of the 85,540 people in the prison population 81,719 are men.

Source:
http://mengage.co.uk/hmp-healthy-male-prisoners/

FACT:

Men get longer sentences for the same crime.

Source:
http://mra-uk.co.uk/?p=215

FACT:

Prisons for women have different rules to those that apply to men.

Source:
https://www.reddit.com/r/MensRights/comments/3vg2ht/why_female_criminals_are_more_likely_than_men_to/

ARE MEN NEVER DISCRIMINATED AGAINST?

FACT:

Before 1861 sex between two men was punishable by hanging.

Before 1967 sex between two men in England and Wales was punishable by prison.

Before 1981 sex between two men in Scotland and Ireland was punishable by prison.

Before 1994 sex between two men was legal if they were over the age of 21.

From 1994 sex between two men was legal if they were over the age of 18 with the age of consent being reduced to 16 in 2001.

In 1954 there were over 1,000 men in prison for being gay (I have to say trying to get a thousand gay men to go 'straight' by denying them access to women and locking them up with a prison full of sex-starved men does not seem to have been the best plan ever).

In contrast, sex between two women has never been illegal and before 2001 there was not even an age of consent.

Source:
https://en.wikipedia.org/wiki/LGBT_rights_in_the_United_Kingdom

THE LAW STILL DISCRIMINATES AGAINST UNMARRIED FATHERS

There have been massive improvements in this but the advice on the government website still starts with the words *"A mother automatically has parental responsibility for her child from birth. A father usually has parental responsibility if he's: …"*

Source:
https://www.gov.uk/parental-rights-responsibilities/who-has-parental-responsibility

This inequity meant that when a mother died in childbirth the father could not take his newborn baby home from hospital without first going to court solely because he was an unmarried father.

Source:
https://brightonmanplan.wordpress.com/2012/03/03/is-it-time-we-curbed-mothers-rights/

I could go on but you get the point.

Jess Phillips's assertion that, *"You hit the jackpot when you are born a boy child."* is at best open to question.

It's very easy to make men look hard-done-by. It's very easy to make women look hard-done-by but if your objective is equality, then it's a mistake to start with the premise that only men or only women are the victims of discrimination.

ARE MEN NEVER DISCRIMINATED AGAINST?

The fight against discrimination is not just a matter of helping oppressed women get there fair share of the jobs, the money and power. True equality cuts both ways and both men and women would have to give up a good deal to achieve it but the good news is that the cost of true equality is far outweighed by the benefits to both men and women with the added bonus of the enormous benefit to children.

By considering only inequality that disadvantages women and by treating inequality as if it were a war against men the 'extreme feminists' with their mantra of "*All men are bastards*" are diverting attention from the real target which is gender inequality regardless or whether it is women, men or as in most cases both who suffer.

Some men and some women discriminate against women. Some men and some women discriminate against men. It's what is going on between their ears that makes them discriminatory not what they have between their legs. The gender of the discriminator is of little or no importance.

A fair society is better for everyone. The reason I have written this book is to take a more balanced look at discrimination and hopefully bring the real reasons for gender inequality into the crosshairs.

If the feminists want to concentrate all their efforts on discrimination that only disadvantages women, well I can live with that, provided it is discrimination and not just men that they are targeting.

EQUALITY FOR WOMEN IS AN OXYMORON

Using discrimination as an excuse to attack all men is misandry plain and simple.

Today almost every aspect of gender discrimination, whether disadvantage or advantage is due to the role separation that our species has used for thousands of years, that is to say, man the provider and woman the carer.

Historically this role separation has always been advantageous to both men and women. Women cannot hunt down large animals as affectively as bigger stronger men and men of course cannot breast feed but the world has changed. Now women can earn the money that brings home the bacon and men can feed the baby with expressed or powdered milk.

It's time for us to move on. Only when the law makers and society stops defining the roles of carer and provider by gender will we achieve equality in the home and in the workplace and then we will see women and men reach their full potential in both these roles.

If your only objective is gender equality then 50% role reversal will achieve this but role reversal with an equal number of men becoming the carer and an equal number of women becoming the provider will not solve the real problem. We will have just as many people chained to the kitchen sink with the rest chained to the office desk or the workbench.

The solution is to share the paid and unpaid work equally between all.

EQUALITY FOR WOMEN IS AN OXYMORON

Chapter 4

Toilet seat syndrome

EQUALITY FOR WOMEN IS AN OXYMORON

Toilet seat syndrome

There was a young man from Crew,
Who left the seat up in the loo.
His wife with a pan,
Reprimanded the man
And now he knows what not to do.

Anonymous

This book is a rewrite of a book previously published as 'Toilet Seat Syndrome'.

Toilet seat syndrome is my shorthand way of describing the phenomenon of unjustified gender discrimination in situations that affect both sexes equally, a classic example of this being the toilet seat.

No man old enough to call himself a man has escaped the wrath of a woman after having left the seat up in the loo at some stage in his life. Men are expected to leave the seat ready for the woman even if she is vastly outnumbered by the men in the house.

Men are told "*It's disrespectful*" or "*It's impolite*" or just plain "*Not acceptable behaviour*" but in truth there is no more reason the man should have to touch the yucky toilet seat than the woman.

Arguments such as, men don't care about yucky stuff, don't

really stand up. Watch the face of a new father changing his first dirty nappy and tell me men don't care about yucky stuff.

The test for equality is simple… You just swap the genders and see if anything changes.

Would a woman still think it reasonable if the genders were reversed and her husband expected her to leave the toilet seat up ready for him, with no suggestion of a reciprocal arrangement?

"Leaving the toilet seat up is the most annoying habit of men, according to a survey of their partners."

According to a questionnaire printed by The Sun newspaper, *"More than half the woman quizzed (54%) said failure to put the seat down was their fella's most irritating trait."*

I can't help thinking that if the toilet seat really is their fella's most irritating trait then they haven't got it so bad.

Source:
http://www.dnaindia.com/lifestyle/report-leaving-the-toilet-seat-up-is-men-s-most-annoying-habit-say-brit-ladies-1427656

If this were only a matter of women being a little bit unreasonable it would be of little importance but the toilet seat is just one small example of how we constantly divide the genders then apply different rules to each.

TOILET SEAT SYNDROME

Consider this MFI advert...

The ad shows a woman in a bathroom. She noticed the toilet seat has been left up and she shouts at her husband to come into the bathroom. When he arrives she shouts, "*You've done it again haven't you? Haven't you?*" and slaps him on the cheek. She then shouts, "*I keep telling you to leave the seat down! I'll spell it out to make it easy for you... D-O-W-N, DOWN!*" she then slaps him again.

The camera pulls back to show that the bathroom is in an MFI showroom. A salesman walks in and puts down the toilet seat and says to the couple "*Ah, I see you have found the soft close toilet seat.*" The voice-over then states, "*When your bathroom's measured, designed and installed by MFI you'll feel right at home.*"

Source:
(In this version of the ad, the slaps have been removed.)
http://www.tellyads.com/play_advert/?filename=TA4063&advertiser=MFI&type=recent

(Here The Mail online shows one of the slaps.)
http://www.dailymail.co.uk/news/article-483921/The-bathroom-ad-slap-landed-MFI-hot-water-trivialising-domestic-violence.html

This advert scores twice on the toilet seat syndrome affect as it suggests it's wrong for a man to leave the seat up but worse than this it also suggests that it's OK for a woman to hit a man.

The advert received hundreds of complaints and was in fact band by the advertising standards agency in September

2007.

The events in this advert are fictitious but it shows that M & C Saatchi at some point thought it was acceptable to use domestic violence to sell bathrooms and to portray domestic violence against a man for comic affect.

Sometimes the 'Toilet Seat Syndrome' effect can lead to inequality or arguments but sometimes it can actually be life or death as with 'man flu'.

Chapter 5

Man flu

EQUALITY FOR WOMEN IS AN OXYMORON

Man flu

"Husband has the sniffles…"

"Can I bring you anything else? Orange juice, tissues, your balls maybe?"

SEEN ON A JOKE CARD

According to Wikipedia the term 'man flu' is described as, *"A pejoratively used phrase that refers to the idea that men, when they have a cold, exaggerate and claim they have the flu."*

The term 'man flu' is normally used in the context of a joke and I like to have a laugh as much as anyone but there is a deadly serious side to this.

Man flu is not about how men deal with illness, it's about how society expects men to deal with illness and far from being wimps who take to their beds at the first sign of a sniffle all the evidence shows that men take too little care of their health and that it is in fact women who make many more visits to the doctor and women also have a lot more sick days off work.

Source:
http://www.healthcareglobal.com/financeinsurance/56/Women-have-more-sick-days-than-men

FACT:

Women live longer than men!

This is in part for physiological reasons but also in part it is because men are reluctant to go and see their doctor. I am not suggesting that the only reason men do not go to the doctor is the fear of ridicule, only that this is a serious problem and that accusations of 'man flu' are a step in the wrong direction and are at best unjustified and at worst lethal.

FACT:

Men who are married live longer than men who are not!

This is thought to be because their wives take charge of their men's health and nag them into going to the doctor when they are ill rather than allowing them to simply ignore their symptoms.

FACT:

Male cancer helplines are used more by women speaking on behalf of partners, fathers or sons, than by the men themselves.

Source:
http://news.bbc.co.uk/2/hi/uk_news/magazine/8154200.stm

MAN FLU

FACT:

More women get skin cancer yet more men die from it. Which suggests that men are leaving it far to long before going to their doctors.

Source:
http://www.itv.com/thismorning/male-cancer-week-helplines

FACT:

Women are almost twice as likely to be diagnosed with depression yet more than three times as many men kill themselves.

Is it possible that the men are simply not being diagnosed and so not getting the help they need?

Source:
https://www.theguardian.com/society/2016/jun/06/women-twice-as-likely-as-men-to-experience-anxiety-research-finds

Telling a man to *"Man up"* when he is ill is wrong and both men and women should stop saying it but accusations of 'man flu' are only a very small part of this problem. With health care it's women that are clearly doing it right and men that are doing it wrong.

We need to get men to change their habits and with the married men living longer thanks to their wives' interventions, women are much more of a help than a hindrance for which we men should be thanking them!

Chapter 6

Gender discrimination in the law

EQUALITY FOR WOMEN IS AN OXYMORON

Gender discrimination in the law

"Men are treated more harshly by the courts than women. For every single category of offence, for all ages and in all types of court, men are more likely to be sent to prison than women. There is not one blip anywhere. For every single offence, for every age, in every type of court, women are less likely to be sent to prison than men."

MP PHIL DAVIES

(Speaking in a debate of female offenders in parliament)

Source:
https://brightonmanplan.wordpress.com/2012/10/20/men-face-sex-discrimination-in-uk-prison-system/

FACT:

Of the 85,540 people in prison 81,719 are men.

Source:
http://mengage.co.uk/hmp-healthy-male-prisoners/

Do women really only commit 5% of all serious crimes?

Discrimination in the criminal justice system is blatant and runs from the first report of a crime right through to sentencing and treatment in prison.

A man and a woman convicted of the same crime can expect very different treatment. A woman will get a much lighter prison sentence if she goes to prison at all.

The government statistics show that, *"Females were (proportionally) more likely to be dealt with out of court for indictable offences compared with males."*

Source:
https://www.gov.uk/government/uploads/system/uploads/attachment_data/file/380090/women-cjs-2013.pdf

In 2013 women received an average prison sentence of 9 months while for men it was 16 months.

Source:
https://www.gov.uk/government/uploads/system/uploads/attachment_data/file/380090/women-cjs-2013.pdf

It's not just that men commit more serious crimes. Men also get longer sentences for the same crime.

Source:
https://www.suffragents.org/women-and-jail

Women also serve 5% less than men, of the sentence they are given.

Source:
http://www.theguardian.com/news/datablog/2013/may/07/men-gender-divide-feminism

Despite this clear gender discrimination all the moves at the moment are towards fewer women in prison and lighter sentences for women.

Source:
http://www.dailymail.co.uk/news/article-1311004/Judges-ordered-mercy-women-criminals-deciding-sentences.html

The Canadian Mounties *"always get their man"* but what if it was a women who did it? Do they just let her go?

The fact that women are more likely to be convicted if arrested has been put forward as evidence of discrimination **against** women in the criminal justice system but I think it much more likely that more women are convicted because they are not being arrested until the evidence is overwhelming.

It is easy to find examples of gender bias in how we react to crimes and whether or not we report them by looking at 'social experiments' online. I have to say here these experiments tend not to be done under scientific conditions and the people doing them often start out to prove what they already believe to be true, however that said, the number of these experiments all showing the same thing, the crime statistics and personal experience leads me to conclude that they are probably about right.

In one such experiment an attractive young woman plays the part of a thief who takes money out of the begging bowl of a sleeping homeless man, played by an actor. People look on in disgust but only one person challenges her actions. The experiment is then repeated with men taking the money and this time 9 out of 10 men are confronted sometimes quite aggressively.

Source:
https://www.youtube.com/watch?v=jUg4Wkty_E4

The same team does a similar experiment but this time they change the gender of the victim. First a woman steals a man's wallet and again only one person challenges her but when a man steals a woman's purse he is always challenged.

Source:
https://www.youtube.com/watch?v=NJGiRXbct40

We also react with gender bias when presented with scenes of violence.

We tend to see the man as the aggressor and the woman as the victim. Minor violence against a woman is considered unacceptable but minor violence against a man is actually laughed at.

In a social experiment conducted in 2014 an argument was staged in a London street with a woman being first shouted at then pushed. Several people, both men and women came to her aid and threatened to call the police.

When the tables are turned and it's the man that is shouted at and pushed around, no one says or does anything, even when the woman grabs his hair and pushes him against some railings the most common reaction especially amongst women is amusement.

Source:
https://www.youtube.com/watch?v=7M0MW6ON484

In these experiments the police were only considered as an option when the victim was a woman.

My conclusion is that proportionately more of the violence against men goes unreported.

Once a crime has been reported do men and women then have a level playing field?

When presented with differing accounts of the facts, do the police and society in general give different weight to the version given by a man or a woman?

In a social experiment a woman accuses a man of pushing her as she walks past. She starts shouting at the man who protests his innocence. A group of men come to her aid and aggressively demand he apologises to the woman. The man continues to protest his innocence but the men threaten to "*beat him up badly.*" In this experiment the men choose to believe the woman and disbelieve the man despite there being no evidence either way.

Source:
https://www.youtube.com/watch?v=xf3Hr3vuB2c

Most extreme is the gender difference when confronted with a serious physical assault between a man and a woman.

In an experiment where a man hits a woman in public, another woman stops and calls him psychotic but when it's the woman doing the hitting the reaction is *"Good for you, you go girl."*

Source:
https://www.youtube.com/watch?v=LlFAd4YdQks

YouTube social experiments are a good way to put a point across however they should be viewed with a degree of caution. We don't know how much was staged, even the bystanders may be actors but if these are indeed accurate representations of how we react then most crimes of theft or violence committed by women go unchallenged and presumably unreported to the police and even when they are reported it's the women who are more likely to be believed. This may go some way to explain the massive 95.5% : 4.5% difference in the male and female prison populations.

In a real life attack, I heard (and believe as a true representation) the story of a man who was arrested for assaulting his wife in a domestic dispute.

The man was arrested and locked in a cell over night without being interviewed.

The next morning, still without hearing the other side of the

GENDER DISCRIMINATION IN THE LAW

story, the man was told his wife and the police intended to press charges against him.

The man was told she had alleged that he had dragged her to the floor and held her there by her neck. The man agreed this was indeed what had happened, an open and shut case... Well not quite.

At this point the police finally asked him for his version of events.

The man explained it was self-defence. He told the police he had managed to stop his wife getting to the carving knife but she had come at him with a saucepan.

With this new information the police decided they would not be able to get a conviction and no further action was taken.

This case is clearly not straightforward. There are probably rights and wrongs on both sides but what I find most interesting is that the police made no attempt to even interview the woman about the man's allegations of what could be an assault with a deadly weapon or even attempted murder.

Is this evidence that the police are institutionally sexist and are simply following the stereotype that in a fight between a man and a woman the man is always the aggressor and the woman always the victim or did they just decide that what was an open and shut case just got too complicated to bother with?

If this case had gone to court it would have been tried under the British criminal justice system, which is often described as the best legal system in the world, but I have my concerns about our great British legal system.

Chapter 7

The law is an ass

EQUALITY FOR WOMEN IS AN OXYMORON

The law is an ass

> "Couldn't help but make me feel ashamed to live in a land where justice is a game."
>
> BOB DYLAN

The British legal system is adversarial.

The defence gives one side of the story and the prosecution presents the other side, then the jury made up of 12 good men and true, decides guilt or innocence. Both sides of the story are presented by highly trained professionals. What could possibly go wrong? Actually plenty...

The first problem is neither the defence nor the prosecution are on the side of truth.

The defence will present you as a God fearing, upstanding pillar of the community. The prosecution will then paint you as the Devil's spawn.

The truth is you are probably neither of these extremes. Both sides are lying and even in the unlikely event that one of them is telling the truth the jury will be none the wiser because their testimony will have been countered by the lies on the other side.

It is not difficult to present a false picture by selectively

EQUALITY FOR WOMEN IS AN OXYMORON

telling the truth...

If I told you that I had seen your daughter out with that Mr Jones and I hear he is often to be seen prancing about in a long black gown and a curly blonde wig, you will probably be thinking this will all end in tears but if I told you that I had seen your daughter out with that Mr Jones, you know, the barrister, you will probably be thinking he will be able to keep my daughter in a manner to which she's completely unaccustomed.

Selectively telling the truth is the biggest lie of all and the bit about telling the whole truth when on oath only seems to apply to the defendant not lawyers or expert witnesses.

Justice is a game and the art of a lawyer is not to present the truth but to twist it to the point of lying while still keeping within the rules of the game. If you can afford a good player of this game your chances of winning go up considerably.

The lawyers on both sides are taught how to discredit a witness regardless of whether their testimony is truthful or not.

A lawyer's training talks of 'witness control', only asking questions you know the answer to, ask closed questions and leading the witness. They are also told to take "baby steps" so if the answer is yes they will ask many questions to ask just one, all ending in "*yes*"... Yes, yes, yes, yes, yes, to the jury it appears as if you have had to answer yes to every question the lawyer has put to you, where as in reality it's just one question broken down.

The lawyer will also look for inconsistencies by asking very similar questions at different times so he may say...

"What was the colour of the car"?

A. *"It was dark, black I think"*

Then later...

Q. *"Can you describe the car"?*

A. *"It was dark blue or black"*

"You previously told the court it was black, now you say it may have been blue, are you not sure?"

The lawyer will then use these minor differences to cast doubt on the credibility of the witness.

The lawyer will also look for any small differences in eye witness accounts and then demand to know if the witness is mistaken or lying.

The truth is, we all remember and experience things differently so there will always be discrepancies and it is in fact the testimonies that match exactly that should be treated with most caution but the lawyer is not concerned with the truth, under the rules of engagement he must do everything he can to win for his side and the benefits for him are considerable. A lawyer with a good reputation can ask for a lot more money and if you are the best in the business you can almost name your price.

Mr Loophole is the name given to Nick Freeman, the defence lawyer who has made a name for himself (and a good deal of money) getting the rich and famous off motoring offences. His unorthodox methods may be appreciated by his clients but if one of the bad drivers he has helped to keep on the road goes on driving badly and kills someone their blood will be on his hands.

My second problem with the British legal system is the jury.

We are told they are 12 good men and true (now includes women of course) but they are made up from the same people you meet in the pub with all their eccentricities, prejudices and sometimes quite bizarre logic, for example…

An ex-girlfriend gave me hell for a week for having an affair. You are probably thinking I got off lightly but there was no affair and the only evidence against me was that all Scorpios were going to have a romantic encounter with a stranger.

That woman maybe sitting on a jury as I write!

With the best will in the world the great British jury do not have the experience needed to see through the skewed version of events presented by both sides or the undermining of truthful witnesses and the down right dirty tricks played by the partisan lawyers.

What is needed is 5 or 7 professional jurors who will have been appointed for their good judgement. They will know the rules of court and will have the experience to know when they are being played by the lawyers. It would also be possible to have jurors with specialist knowledge in certain areas for some of the more complex cases.

My third problem with the British legal system is the pressures put on defendants to plead guilty…

In far too many cases it is not the judge or the jury that decide the outcome but the defendant along with their lawyer. They will assess the likely verdict and if it looks as if they may be found guilty then the defendant may be advised to make a guilty plea. This will deny an innocent man his day in court but the advantages are many.

A guilty plea will give a defendant (innocent or guilty) the opportunity to plea bargain, he can offer to plead guilty to a lesser offence and save every one the bother and cost of a long drawn out trial.

A guilty plea will automatically get the defendant a reduced sentence.

A guilty plea means the defendant can be considered for parole where as a man who continues to protest his innocence may not always be considered for parole as he has yet to show remorse.

There have been many instances of men staying in prison rather than admit their guilt, for instance...

The murder of Linda Cook was committed in Portsmouth on 9 December 1986. The subsequent trial led to a miscarriage of justice when Michael Shirley, an 18-year-old Royal Navy sailor, was wrongly convicted of the crime and sentenced to life imprisonment.

After serving the minimum 15 years, Shirley would have been released from prison had he confessed to the killing and shown remorse to the parole board, but he refused to do so and said: "*I would have died in prison rather than admit to something I didn't do. I was prepared to stay in forever if necessary to prove my innocence.*" Shirley's conviction was eventually quashed by the Court of Appeal in 2003, on the basis of exculpatory DNA evidence.

DNA can prove guilt but it can also prove innocence.

The innocence project in the USA has used DNA to re-look at cases that were tried before DNA was available. Of the 347 released after the DNA proved their innocence 36 had pleaded guilty, that's over 10% wrongly convicted of mostly rapes and murders because when given the choice of pleading not guilty and probably going to prison for a long time or pleading guilty and definitely going to prison for a shorter time they chose the shorter sentence.

Source:
http://www.innocenceproject.org/dna-exonerations-in-the-united-states/

Many people accept a caution for something that would never stand up in a court of law, believing that it's just a telling off from the police and not worth defending.

A police caution is not a conviction but you have to admit your guilt and you do get a police record that will show up on a Criminal Records Bureau check.

In 2015 there were 153,000 cautions revealed on CRB checks that were made by people applying for jobs or university places.

FACT:

The caution you received when you were 13 years old will stay on your record for the next 87 years!

Source:
http://www.dailymail.co.uk/news/article-2227522/Police-cautions-lead-100-year-criminal-record-wreck-prospects-getting-job-going-university.html

My fourth problem with the British legal system is the cost...

For the man in the street the cost of legal redress is so expensive that it's not really an option and even for those who can afford to go to court, the outcome will vary depending on the amount he can afford to spend on his legal team.

Something is very very wrong with the justice system when the quality of the lawyer is more important than the quality of the evidence!

Example…

I knew two men who had the same problem at the same time, I will call them Bill and Ben. Both men were being denied access to their children.

Bill was being denied access to his children by his ex, as a punishment for the divorce. Going to court cost him thousands and took almost a year, (his ex had legal aid).

On the day of the hearing, at the very last moment on the steps of the court the solicitors did what they should have done in the first place, they agreed access but because this was just a verbal agreement not a court judgement it was not legally binding.

After a couple of weeks Bill's access had gone right back to "if or when his ex felt like it."

Bill had to start the process again at great expense and with more of his children's lives spent without the benefits and stability of a good access agreement. This process is far too long and far too expensive.

Ben on the other hand took a different route…

When Ben's ex told him he was no longer allowed to phone every week and that actual contact was to be reduced to almost zero, Ben asked why. He was told her new partner didn't like the unavoidable contact she had with Ben when answering the phone or the door.

Ben's response was swift and to the point. *"Tell him that access to my kids is the only thing keeping him alive."* The implication being that without the threat of a restraining order stopping Ben from seeing his children at all, there was no longer a good enough reason not to take revenge on her new partner. The result was instant, full access was restored.

I am not advocating threats to resolve access disputes but the adversarial legal option is not the answer either. The only just, affordable and workable answer is binding mediation.

My fifth problem with the British legal system is that it is discriminatory.

The criminal justice system is not just sexist, but ageist, racist and elitist, with a hugely disproportionate amount of poor young black men locked up.

The law is elitist...

The first thing your lawyer will tell you when going to court is to wear a suit and if you can speak with a plummy accent so much the better.

The ability to buy a good defence also helps of course.

The law is sexist...

It's sexist as described in the chapter 'Gender discrimination in the law' but also in divorce cases it's often only one side (usually the woman) that gets legal aid however with the introduction of new rules for divorce very few people of either gender will now get legal aid unless there has been violence.

I predict this change will lead to a massive increase in allegations of violence in divorce cases and if there is indeed an increase in false claims of violence for financial reasons this will have the added affect of unfairly influencing custardy and access decisions to the detriment of children, fathers and to a lesser extent mothers.

There have been massive improvements in the law since the turn of the 21st century...

Since 2001 Gay men now have the same age of consent as gay women.

Since 2003 unmarried fathers have gone from having no rights at all to having almost as many rights as unmarried mothers.

Since 2009 male rape is now a crime in all parts of the UK.

Source:
http://www.scotland.police.uk/whats-happening/campaigns/2014/we-can-stop-it-rape-awareness
http://www.youngstonewall.org.uk/lgbtq-info/legal-equality
https://www.gov.uk/parental-rights-responsibilities/who-has-parental-responsibility

The law is racist…

If you are black or Asian you are three times more likely to be arrested, you are more likely to be sent to prison and you can expect a longer sentence.

Source:
http://www.theguardian.com/law/2011/nov/25/ethnic-variations-jail-sentences-study
http://www.irr.org.uk/research/statistics/criminal-justice/

My sixth problem with the British legal system is the 'claims culture' that has grown up in the UK.

The prospect of large payouts will inevitably lead to some false claims. Claims for accidents and falls are already increasing the cost of insurance for all of us.

The extent of the fraud is so great that it's estimated that the new rules on whiplash injuries alone will save us £50 each on our car insurance but much more important than that is the miscarriages of justice that must surely come with the enticement of huge payouts for historic sex abuse and pedophilia.

Source:
http://www.bbc.com/news/uk-35188305

The level of proof required for a payout from the estate of Jimmy Savile is very low and with the number of claimants now at over 200 it's likely that some of these are fraudulent.

No one is going to get too upset if a prolific pedophile is robbed by fraudsters but that is not what is going to happen. Savile is dead, he can loose nothing but the lawyers are not just going after Savile's estate they also have their hands in the much deeper pockets of the NHS and the BBC.

If we want to prevent the NHS, BBC and charities being robbed by fraudsters we need to scrutinise every claim before paying out but this will actually cost them more of our money.

The option we are given here is not, do we pay all compensation claims (some of which may be fraudulent), or do we keep the much-needed money in the NHS. The option is do we pay all compensation claims (some of which may be fraudulent), or do we pay even more in legal costs.

This looks more like extortion than justice.

Source:
http://www.bbc.com/news/uk-28558442

EQUALITY FOR WOMEN IS AN OXYMORON

Chapter 8

What part of "No!" do you not understand?

EQUALITY FOR WOMEN IS AN OXYMORON

What part of "No!" do you not understand?

I LIKE THE GIRLS THAT DO

*I like the girls who do.
I like the girls who don't.
I hate the girl who says she will
and then she says she won't.
But the girl I like best of all,
and I think you'll say I'm right,
is the girl who says she never does
but she looks as though she might*

MAX MILLER

If Max Miller were to 'chat up the girls that say they never do, is he an optimist or a sex pest?

Things have changed since the days of Max Miller. Now if a man as much as looks at a woman he may be accused of sexual harassment or stare rape but if we demonise all men for even the slightest hint of sexual interest and vilify all women with words like slut and whore, then who is allowed to make the first move?

Of course women should not have to fight off unwanted sexual advances at work, on the street or anywhere else and neither should men.

There is a solid line between acceptable and unacceptable behaviour that none of us should ever cross but this uncrossable line is not fixed and the very survival of our species requires both men and women to sometimes move so far across the line of what was accepted behaviour for strangers, that they actually have sex.

Gone are the days, (if they ever existed) when your first kiss was not until you had been given permission to kiss the bride on your wedding day. Today to get to the point where two strangers become a mating pair, humans must go through an elaborate mating ritual during which the line marking the point at which behaviour is considered acceptable is constantly being moved.

To stay on the 'acceptable behaviour' side of this line, both parties must correctly interpret the signals put out by the other. The only problem is that this requires everyone to know exactly what everyone else wants and to confuse the young and inexperienced even more, they are often getting mixed messages.

On the one hand a young man is told that if he tells a woman at work she looks nice, she may make a complaint of sexual harassment or say that she is being objectivised while at the same time Bonnie Tyler is *"Holding out for a hero to sweep her of her feet"* and Lily Allen is waiting for *"the man of her dreams to come along, pick her up and put her over his shoulder"* and then there is '50 shades of grey' and the whole bodice ripper genre of books. These books are written

WHAT PART OF "NO!" DO YOU NOT UNDERSTAND?

by women for women and are all based around non-consensual sex and that's not the villain, that's the hero.

How many times will the quiet man watch Bonnie and Lily walk out with the more proactive competition before he starts to think nice guys really do finish last and decide to rethink his strategy?

How does an inexperienced man know…

When a woman is just **playing** hard to get?

When a woman is just **acting** coy?

When is a woman saying no because she doesn't want you to think she is too easy or a slut?

The Internet is full of advice for girls on how to act coy to **increase** her chances of getting her man but when using such ploys the girl must, "say she never does but look as if she might." She must say no when she actually means yes.

When playing hard to get a woman may quite justifiably be testing the seriousness of the man's intentions. If he is only after a quick fling or a one night stand then she will quickly find this out and move on to the next candidate in her search for Mr Right but if we accept that human mating rituals include saying one thing while meaning another then some misunderstandings are inevitable.

The part of "No" some men are having trouble with is that "No" means whatever the woman wants it to mean and this varies from woman to woman or the same woman at different times or with different men.

Depending on the situation, "No" can mean "No" or "Maybe" or "Try harder", or even "Yes"!

When in my late teens I met a girl, we chatted and had a few drinks all seemed to be going well. I invited her to come back to my place for a… 'euphemistic coffee' but she said no, so under the rules of no means no, I chalked this one up to experience and went home alone.

A week or so later I saw this girl again only this time she was on the arm of another man. When he went up to the bar, she came over to me and whispered in my ear "*You know you shouldn't have given up so easily the other night, I was on the point of giving in.*" It seems that sometimes no can indeed mean try harder, the problem for men is deciding when!

A woman has the right to say "No" at any time. On this I think we are all agreed.

A woman has the right to say no right up to the last minute.

She can say…

"Yes, yes, yes, OH YES! - NO!" and he must stop!

WHAT PART OF "NO!" DO YOU NOT UNDERSTAND?

If, as we are so often told "It's a woman's prerogative to change her mind" then how can a young man be sure a woman who is saying "No" won't change her mind and say "Yes"? How does a young man know she won't say "No, no, no, - oh go on then"?

A woman not only has the right to say no at the very last minute, but under the golden rule of sex, which is **No one does anything they don't want to**, if she no longer wants to continue she MUST say so and he MUST stop!

The woman's right to say no at the very last minute brings with it the responsibility to make sure that as far as possible she never needs to use it.

A woman may find a man's attentions flattering but it is not fair for her to give him false hope by flirting or by accepting gifts, these are steps in the mating game and the sooner she makes her intentions clear the easier it will be for all concerned.

Girls also apply their own rules when dating. If they don't want to appear too keen or worse still, a slut, they will have probably already decided how far they want to go on a first date. If a girl finds she is sexually aroused by her date but has decided to go no further than a peck on the cheek she may be sending out mixed messages.

When a woman is sexually aroused her whole body changes, dilation of the pupils, reddening of the lips and cheeks etc, she will also send out subliminal messages with her body language, by touching her hair, licking her lips, or batting her eyelashes.

It is perfectly normal for a girl to be both sexually aroused but still saying no. In such cases her head may be telling her to say no thank you, while her heart through her body language might be saying yes please! Such mixed messages can be confusing for an inexperienced young man to interpret.

I am not suggesting that this ambiguity is the cause of most sexual assaults, most girls make their intentions very clear but I do think a lot of men would not cross the line between flirting and pestering and then on to sexual harassment if the line were more clearly defined and fixed but it doesn't work like that.

The problem is that the difference between flirting and pestering is often just a matter of who is doing the flirting or pestering and what is going on in the woman's head.

A woman who is wearing a skirt up to here and a top cut down to there, with blusher, lipstick and eye make-up is sending out a very clear message but it is not intended for the middle-aged cab driver who has just adjusted his rear view mirror to get a better look at his fare.

The cabby knows he is not the young woman's intended target. All her efforts are to impress some young hunk of a

WHAT PART OF "NO!"
DO YOU NOT UNDERSTAND?

man who is waiting at the bar that he is driving her to.

There is no confusion here, she doesn't need to wear a sign saying "Look at me, but only if you are tall dark and handsome!" The middle-aged cabby knows it's not him she dressed up for but it's not always quite so clear.

What if the cabby were younger or the woman older? Should he let the woman of his dreams just get out of his cab or should he say something and if he does will he get a date, or the sack?

The answer to this depends entirely on what is in the mind of the woman but it is not acceptable for the cabby to come right out and ask her. This could lead to complaints of harassment. Instead he must look for clues in what she says and does. Is she laughing, giggling, flirting, touching her hair, touching his arm, giving him the eye, fluttering her eyelashes, etc, etc and if so should he risk his job and rejection or play it safe and drive away?

Consider this scenario…

Do you remember the TV ad for jeans where a drop dead gorgeous hunk strips seductively down to his underwear in a launderette, he puts his clothes in the washing machine, while some women look on admiringly?

Source:
https://www.youtube.com/watch?v=wT4DR_ae_4o

Now run the ad again but with a dirty old tramp in place of the hunk. The tramp has no washing machine and only owns one set of clothes so if he is to wash his dirty clothes, he has no option but to strip off in the launderette.

Today, if a hunk were to strip off in a launderette the girls would take out their phones to film him but if a tramp stripped off they would be using their phones to call the police!

The actions of the men are the same but the reactions of the women are very different depending **only** on how attractive they find the men and the only one that knows that for sure is the woman herself. Each man can only make an educated guess as to the woman's reaction based on his previous experience.

The TV ad was some time ago and for all we know the hunk is now a middle-aged, pot-bellied taxi driver.

I suggest the point at which he switched from being a flirt to being a sex pest would have been very gradual. He would not have gone from Greek god to couch potato over night and there would have been many years where he was neither one thing nor the other and during this time the acceptability of his behaviour would have become even more of a judgement call, with some women pleased, while others are outraged.

The old way of finding out where a particular woman (or

WHAT PART OF "NO!" DO YOU NOT UNDERSTAND?

sometimes the man) had drawn the uncrossable line was for the man (or sometimes the woman) to gently push against the line by flirting and then look for the reaction. If he felt resistance then he has found her line, if not then he can move things on little by little until he has the confidence to suggest a date.

If you ask someone of middle age or older where they met their spouse they are very likely to say, "*At work*" but things have changed now. To protect themselves and their staff, most employers forbid even the slightest suggestion of flirting so how are the parents of the next generation going to get together?

The new way seems to be, to involve a third party.

'Boy meets girl' should now read, 'Boy and girl go online, clearly state what they want and what they expect then review the profiles of the other men or women in search of love, select the most likely candidate for Mr or Miss Right and hope for a match'. This is the modern version of being formally introduced to someone suitable who you now have permission to flirt with.

It may not be as romantic as eyes meeting across a crowded room but it may well be the only way round the impasse of the man can't make the first move for fear of being labeled a sex pest and the woman can't make the first move for fear of being labeled a slut.

Once both parties have established an interest, the "mating game" still has to be played and for this to be done successfully everyone needs to be playing by the same rules.

As they approach puberty, we need to teach our children accepted and understood ways of saying, "Yes", "No" or "Maybe". We need to give them the tools to navigate the hormonal storm that is coming their way.

Phrases like "I love you like a sister" or "I love you as a friend" can be used to gently say I am not interested in a sexual relationship but **they must be clear**.

The very first website I looked at when researching this chapter was called 'How to say No to a boy'.

This site suggests that, to say No, girls should say they are not interested **right now** and give him a friendly hug.

This will definitely give him false hope.

Source:
http://www.wikihow.com/Say-No-to-a-Boy

It's not necessary to be vicious to be clear.

The girl who looked the boy up and down then mimicked putting her fingers down her throat to make herself sick or when offered his best chat-up line sneered and said "*Oh a funny cunt*" was clear but unnecessarily hurtful. He may not

WHAT PART OF "NO!" DO YOU NOT UNDERSTAND?

be her Mr Right but he is someone's and she may now never get asked.

It's not the odd small misunderstanding that is the problem, it's the momentum that can build up and become almost unstoppable.

In the world of S and M (sadomasochism) "No" quite often means yes so they use "safe words" for when they really do want to stop. We in the world of 'normal' sex need to do the same.

If we all know and use words like "Amber Light" for too much, too fast and "Red Light" for stop perhaps we can halt the snowball that if unchecked can easily become an avalanche.

I have a suggestion that would make the woman's position crystal clear when things start going badly wrong!

If the man is not getting the message then instead of continuing to say no or use safe words the woman should use the word "*rape.*" If she said something like "*If you don't stop now it will be rape*" or "*What will your mother say when she knows you raped me*" there can be no possibility of any misunderstanding.

Most men are not rapists and would be horrified to think anyone thought that they were. Just the word "rape" invokes a feeling of revulsion in all right minded people and this is a powerful weapon that women can use to shock a man into realising he has gone too far.

When a woman uses the word 'rape' it is no longer possible for a man to convince himself that the woman is just playing hard to get and wants it really.

If a man continues after such a clear message there can be no doubt, it is rape, he is a rapist and not interested in whether she consents or not. At this point the only advantage she will have gained from using the word rape is that it will clarify what happened if or hopefully when it goes to court.

Chapter 9

Rape

EQUALITY FOR WOMEN IS AN OXYMORON

Rape

> *"If I leave a window open an inch and someone breaks in steals everything I own and ransacks my house no one would say it wasn't a crime or that the offender had 'made a mistake."*
>
> HARRIET HARMAN

If a woman is too drunk to give her consent then it's rape but this is not a very good analogy.

When a woman is wearing very little and deliberately gets blind drunk, it's more like piling all your valuables in front of the window, then leaving it wide open with a note saying no one is home until morning.

If someone then breaks in and steals everything you own it's still a crime, he is still a thief but you are not likely to get paid out on your insurance because you didn't do enough to keep your property safe.

If the police set up such a house to try and catch a thief they would struggle to get a conviction even if they caught him in the act because it would be classed as incitement.

Rape is never the victim's fault but we do those at risk a huge disservice if we don't tell them there is a lot they can do to stay safer.

If our objective is to reduce the number of rapes it's not enough to catch and convict as many rapists as possible we also need to do everything we can to not become a victim.

The Sexual Offences Act 2003 defines the elements of rape as:

> (A) intentionally penetrates the vagina, anus or mouth of another person (B) with his penis;

> (B) does not consent to the penetration and (A) does not reasonably believe that (B) consents.

For a rape to take place there must be penetration with a penis making rape an exclusively male crime with the only exception being where a woman aids a man to commit rape in which case both the man and the woman can be convicted of rape.

Rape comes in many different forms...

I had a friend who repeatedly had unintended sex with someone when far too drunk to give consent. The genders are the wrong way round for it to be rape but the circumstances are the same so I am going to use the word anyway.

My friend was raped many times, over a long period. He was not held captive or threatened and at the time his friends, myself included did not consider it rape. What

RAPE

happened was this...

When in our late teens and early twenties my friends and I would go out on what is now called binge drinking. One of our number was a bit older than us and had a couple of kids but most importantly for us, he also had a house, so after the pubs closed we would go back to his place to carry on drinking.

While we were out our friend's children were looked after by a middle-aged woman who lived a few doors away. When we rolled in drunk as always, one of my friends would make a b-line for the babysitter. He would burst in through the door, arms outstretched slurring *"Hello my darling"* engulfing her in a wobbly embrace and smothering her in kisses. This would all end with them sleeping together.

I know this is not what he wanted when he was sober because before the drinking started he would put his arms round our shoulders and say, *"Listen lads whatever happens tonight don't let me sleep with the babysitter!"*

He was drunk so was not capable of giving consent, she was sober so he was clearly raped but what is not clear is how hard she needed to fight off his attempts to have sex with her before the tables turned and she became the victim and he became the rapist.

At the time it all seemed straightforward. It never even

occurred to us that a crime might have been committed. It was his own silly fault. Unintended sex is one of the many risks you take when you go out and get blind drunk.

If the ages and genders had been reversed and a drunk 20 year old woman had come home and had unintended sex with a middle-aged man would we have felt the same and just consider it her own silly fault?

On reflection I think my friend and the babysitter were each responsible for their own actions. A person who is mentally ill is not responsible for their actions but a person such as my friend who deliberately put themselves in a position of mental incapacity through drink or drugs remain responsible for their actions while in that state whether it is unintended sex, driving under the influence, or vomiting in the back of a taxi, however none of this absolves the babysitter of her responsibility to make certain that my friend was capable of giving consent which he clearly was not.

No action was ever taken for what happened and I think that was probably the best outcome for what would have clearly been rape if the genders were reversed albeit at the very mildest end of the scale and I doubt whether anyone suffered enough to make it in the public interest to pay the cost of an investigation and trial.

At the other end of the scale I knew a girl (she was under 18) who was raped in the most horrible way imaginable.

RAPE

The girl went to a party with her boyfriend. They went upstairs and had consensual sex, then in an act of bravado he went down stairs and told his Hell's Angel friends, *"I've finished now if anyone else wants a go..."* They all did.

They held her down hit her and all took turns. When they had finished with her they took all her clothes as trophies leaving her to walk home from the party with only a coat that another girl had lent her.

I didn't know her until about a year after this happened but at the time she would have been about 16 possibly younger. When I last saw her she would have been in her mid twenties by which time thankfully the nightmares had all but stopped but I doubt she will ever recover fully from what they did to her.

I am no apologist for rape! If the men that gang raped my friend were sentenced to life I would be among those cheering from the public gallery as they took them down to the cells but since the attack took place a long time ago and like so many rapes it was never reported the chance of these men ever facing a trial is virtually zero.

My point is that rape is not always the same and the best way to prevent or reduce it also varies.

The offence of rape is not about the use of force. Many rapes take place without violence or threats of violence and many couples enjoy a good deal of violence while having consensual sex perfectly legally.

The crime of rape ranges from a violent attack, that is life ending either through murder or suicide to the other extreme where neither the victim nor the rapist realise an offence has been committed.

Rape can be:

The stranger in the alley. This accounts for only around 10% of rapes. Most victims know their attacker before the attack.

Source:
http://rapecrisis.org.uk/statistics.php

If a woman walks alone down a dark alley she risks being raped, mugged or murdered. If a man walks alone down a dark alley he also risks being raped, mugged or murdered.

The woman is more likely to get raped than the man is but the man is more likely to get murdered than she is. The safest thing for both men and women is to stay away from high risk places.

It's not fair that law-abiding men and women are excluded from walking where they please by murderers and rapists but it's far better than the alternative.

When car manufacturers improved the security on their cars the rate of theft went down by 70%. If we can make life harder for the rapists we should take every opportunity to do so.

Source:
http://www.telegraph.co.uk/finance/newsbysector/transport/11558743/Number-of-cars-stolen-in-the-UK-falls-to-48-year-low.html

Rape can be:

A group of men (may also include women) who get a mob or heard mentality and do things they would never have thought themselves capable of.

The herd mentality takes many forms - it can be rioters, looters, football hooligans, bullies, the mob who kick a man to death, lynchings or gang rapes.

What these all have in common is that their actions are encouraged or at least not condemned by their peers. The herd mentality has it's own momentum which rapidly escalates with all it's members acting out of character.

The herd mentality transforms a bunch of ordinary people into a mob, who look back the next morning, not understanding what happened, shocked and disgusted by their own actions but by then it's too late, the damage is done.

The herd mentality probably lies dormant in all of us and at its height it can become almost unstoppable. The time to act is before it picks up momentum. We need to stop it before it starts.

If we learn to recognise the signs, the perpetrators will have a chance to stop and the victims will have a chance to get to a place of safety before things get too out of hand.

Rape can be:

When a man slips ketamine (one of the date rape drugs) into the victim's drink.

It is far easier to convict someone who uses drugs to rape because the prosecution will rely on the evidence of what was actually done rather than what was going on in the minds of the victim and the perpetrator.

If a man goes out equipped to rape with ketamine in his pocket then his crime was clearly premeditated and the police can look for traces of the drug in the victim and the purchase history between the accused and the dodgy online pharmacy that sold him the drug.

It's ironic that if the rapist used a condom and there was no pregnancy and no STDs then the victim might be completely unaware of the rape, in which case the victim will only suffer the trauma of having been raped when he or she is made aware of it by the police or a friend.

Rape can be:

RAPE

When the victim has gone as far as she or he wants to, but the rapist is not taking "No" for an answer.

Humans go through an elaborate mating ritual that starts with flirting and ends in sex. If a woman flirts, accepts gifts and invites a man in for coffee this does not necessarily mean it will end in sex but this may well be how it's interpreted by the man.

TRUE STORY:

I once knew two girls who would play a game, competing with each other. The rules were to go out with only the price of one drink and see what you could get men to buy for you. On a bad night they would get very drunk, on a good night they would get drunk and then on to a Chinese or Indian restaurant.

In the words of The Kinks *"He'd end up blowing all his wages for the week, all for a cuddle and a peck on the cheek."*

This is a dangerous game to play. If a woman leads a man on then drops him, she will create a storm of emotions including lust, love, anticipation, rejection, frustration, humiliation and anger. None of which excuses rape but does greatly increase it's probability.

Rape can be:

Where the victim is an enthusiastic participant but under the age of consent.

I knew a woman who was raped at the age of 14 by her 20 year old boyfriend and I recently read an oral history called 'Eight London Lives' by Mike Turner, in which a woman recounts how at 14 year old she was also raped by her 20 year old boyfriend.

In both cases the girls were enthusiastic participants but too young to give their consent and therefore both girls were raped.

In both cases the girls got pregnant.

In both cases the girls refused to give the father's name (this was before DNA tests).

In both cases the girls then married the father as soon as they were old enough.

The woman I knew divorced 5 years and 2 more children later.

The woman in the book is still happily married to this day some 60 years later.

Sex between a 20 year old man and a 14 year old girl is clearly wrong, everyone can see that. Everyone except the girls that is, they never thought of the men as rapists or themselves as victims.

RAPE

Rape can be:

The students, waking up, the morning after the night before, looking at the person they find themselves in bed with and thinking, oh god I didn't did I?

Too drunk to consent means it's rape but in this scenario who is the rapist?

You can't answer this question with the limited information I have given here but what else do you need to know? Do you need to know who did what, who was thinking what at the time or just what gender they were?

If it's the latter then this is clearly not a gender blind law.

Rape can be:

The undercover policeman who wasn't who he said he was.

Source:
https://www.theguardian.com/commentisfree/2013/jun/28/sexual-behaviour-undercover-police

If a woman is passionate about a cause, she is far more likely to choose a man who shares her passion.

An animal rights activist is unlikely to sleep with an undercover policeman who's job it is, to stop her and her friends committing illegal acts to protect animals, unless she doesn't know that's who he is, in which case his deception will void her consent.

The law says a woman needs to know who it is she is consenting to have sex with before she can give her consent but men bend the truth and lie all the time to impress a prospective sexual partner, as do women but at what point does 'talking yourself up' become deception?

What if a man buys himself a cheap fake Rolex and pretends it's real, is that deception?

What if a woman knocks ten years off her age, changes the colour of her eyes with coloured contact lenses and stuffs her bra with tissues, is that deception?

What about the men and women who quietly slip off their wedding rings and forget to mention their children who will have a prior claim on their time, their income and their emotions?

What of the women who are already pregnant and just looking for a man to pin the blame on?

What of the men who swear undying love then disappear in the morning or the women that are only really interested in his money?

What of transgender? If a man wants to legally change his gender all he needs to do is live as a woman for two years but is a frock and a piece of paper really all it would take to convince a straight man to have sex with him/her?

Your gender is written into your DNA no amount of hormones or surgery can change that.

If a man or woman has had gender reassignment surgery at what point should they tell a new boy/girlfriend?

- Before the first date?
- Before the first kiss?
- Before sex?
- Never?

Rape can be:

When a man doesn't do what he said he would do.

If a man agrees to withdraw before ejaculation or wear a condom but does not, then that is rape. A woman or man who finds out they have been lied to after enjoying what they believed to be consensual sex has certainly been wronged but they are unlikely to feel the same level of violation and trauma as the person who was held down or terrified into compliance.

For a woman or man to give that consent she/he needs to have...

The freedom to make a choice without coercion;

She/he must have the capacity to make a choice;

She/he needs to know what she/he is consenting to;

She/he needs to know who it is she/he is consenting to have sex with.

The freedom to make a choice is obviously necessary for any consent but the capacity is more difficult to define. For a law to work affectively everyone needs to be clear about what is and what is not legal.

An under age child or a person with the mental age of an under age child does not have the capacity to give consent that is clear but what of a person who is intoxicated by alcohol or affected by drugs? At what point does the alcohol void their consent?

In the case of R vs Bree the Court of Appeal explored the issue of capacity and consent, stating that…

"If, through drink, or for any other reason, a complainant had temporarily lost her capacity to choose whether to have sexual intercourse, she was not consenting and subject to the defendant's state of mind, if intercourse took place, that would be rape."

However…

"Where a complainant had voluntarily consumed substantial quantities of alcohol, but nevertheless remained capable of choosing whether to have intercourse and agreed

to do so, that would not be rape." Further, they identified that *"Capacity to consent may evaporate well before a complainant becomes unconscious. Whether this is so or not, however, depends on the facts of the case."*

So before I go out on the pull tonight can we just clarify this?

A woman who has voluntarily consumed substantial quantities of alcohol may remain capable of consent but her consent may evaporate well before she becomes unconscious. This requires me to make a judgement call for which I will need to know...

> How much she has drunk (did she pre-load on cheap supermarket vodka before she came out)?
>
> Over what period of time did she consume the alcohol? (Her body may have already metabolised her earlier drinks).
>
> How much does she normally drink (a woman that habitually knocks back a bottle of spirits every day will not be affected in the same way as a woman who is drinking for the first time).
>
> At what point a judge would consider her capacity to consent to have evaporated?

I must do this while my own judgement is also impaired by

drink.

If I get it right, a good time will be had by all, but get it wrong and I will be branded a rapist with up to life imprisonment and my name on the sex offender's register!

If the laws are worded too loosely then bad or even normal behaviour becomes rape and from there, rape will loose it's stigma and it's the universal revulsion at even the word rape that is the best protection women and men have (1 in 7 rape victims are men).

So how can we reduce the number of rapes?

If our objective is only to increase the conviction rate for rape then the promise to be believed and the promise of life long anonymity will help to do this but more convictions should not be our starting point.

Our primary aim should be to reduce as far as possible the number of rapes and locking up rapists is only one weapon in our arsenal.

There is no golden bullet that will end rape so when trying to reduce the number of rapes we must have a multiple attack. Understanding the series of events that may end in rape will help victims and also perpetrators avoid their consequences.

If we tell girls from an early age to use the word 'rape' when 'no' is not getting through and if we tell boys that if they don't stop when a girl uses that word then they will become a rapist, despised by everyone and sentenced to life imprisonment then I think all ambiguity and at least some of the rapes may be avoided.

When you loose your mind to drink you put yourself at risk. The time to assess this risk is before you start drinking.

For some people (men and women), their weekend 'to do list' reads...

>Go out;
>
>Get drunk;
>
>Get laid.

For the shy and the timid, alcohol may be the Dutch courage needed to even talk to the opposite sex but if sex is not what you want then before you loose your mind to drink you need to be sure you are with people who know this and people you can trust.

Mob mentality relies on peer approval but this cuts both ways. Peer disapproval can be an equally strong force to stop rape and it is this that is harnessed in the green dot project.

Source:
https://rsvp.missouri.edu/whats-with-the-green-dot/

Finding, convicting and locking away rapists will reduce the number of rapes but only if we lock-away the right man. Locking away the wrong man will actually make the situation worse.

Chapter 10

False rape claims

EQUALITY FOR WOMEN IS AN OXYMORON

False rape claims

"It is a myth that victims cry rape when they regret having sex or want revenge, and prosecutors who deal with rape cases are taught about such myths as part of their specialist training."

CPS (Criminal Prosecution Service)

The damage of falsely claiming rape ranges from life destroying to life ending either through suicide or even murder yet there are calls to never prosecute men or women who falsely cry rape.

Women Against Rape (WAR) claim there are far too many prosecutions for false rape allegations and that this is not in line with other countries. The number of rape prosecutions in 2012/13 was 3,692 and the average number of prosecutions for false rape claims were 22.

WAR use the case of Eleanor de Freitas, a rape complainant who killed herself on the eve of prosecution for perverting the course of justice as a justification for never prosecuting any false rape claims. Presumably given the number of men who kill themselves when accused of rape (both guilty and innocent) WAR will also be against the prosecution of those accused of rape or any other serious crime for fear they may also kill themselves.

WAR also claim prosecuting women for false rape

allegations violates their human rights.

Source:
https://www.theguardian.com/law/2014/dec/01/109-women-prosecuted-false-rape-allegations
https://www.theguardian.com/commentisfree/2014/dec/02/britain-violating-rape-victims-human-rights

When discussing false rape I use the word complainant or accuser to describe the person making the accusation. In most statements concerning false rape the complainant is still described as the victim, this is confusing because in rape, the victim is the person who has been raped but in false rape allegations the victim is the man who has been falsely accused.

The CPS statement, *"It is a myth that victims cry rape when they regret having sex or want revenge"* is quite simply wrong.

A myth is something that does not exist. False rape claims do exist and the CPS know they exist. They prosecute 22 people for it every year.

The question is not do people ever lie about being raped, the question is: Which of the thousands of rapes that are reported are true and how many of them are false accusations?

Charles P. McDowell, a researcher in the United States Air Force Special Studies Division, studied the 1,218 reports of rape that were made between 1980 and 1984 on Air Force bases throughout the world.

McDowell found that 460 were found to be "proven" allegations, either because the "overwhelming preponderance of the evidence" supported the allegation or because there was a conviction in the case. Another 212 of the total reports were found to be "disproved" as the alleged victim convincingly admitted the complaint was a 'hoax' at some point during the initial investigation.

The researchers then investigated the 546 remaining or 'unresolved' rape allegations including having the accusers submit to a polygraph (lie detector test). 27% of these complainants admitted they had fabricated their accusation just before taking the polygraph or right after they failed the test. Whenever there was any doubt, the unresolved case was re-classified as a proven rape.

Combining this 27% with the initial 212 'disproved' cases, it was determined that approximately 45% of the total rape allegations were false.

The figure of 45% seems too high to be credible but we must remember that many genuine cases of rape go unreported while all the false rape claims are by definition reported, so if only 1 in 3 genuine rapes are reported then the number of false rapes compared to the number of genuine rapes is actually 15%. This seems much more realistic but the police will still be faced with almost half the rape accusations they see being false.

If this research is correct and it has to be said that this is just one relatively small sample then investigators clearly need to keep an open mind when deciding who is telling the truth.

Source:
http://human-stupidity.com/stupid-dogma/mens-rights-feminism/rapists-proven-innocent-are-majority-57-of-prisoners-released-by-innocence-project

The innocence project was set up in the USA to review old criminal convictions using new DNA techniques. Of the 268 exonerations so far 153 were for rape and over 10% of the wrongly convicted had pleaded guilty, presumably to reduce the length of their incorrect sentence.

Source:
http://www.avoiceformen.com/mens-rights/false-rape-culture/register-her-com-goes-worldwide/

The innocence project proves beyond any doubt that in some cases an allegation of rape against a man is wrong and that a presumption of guilt with the promise that all victims will be believed is not a safe way to conduct an investigation but why would a woman or a man claim to have been raped if it were not true?

The most common reasons are…

Alibi; Revenge; Attention seeking; Regret; Money; Empowerment; Character assassination (in politics or

other); Solidarity and Mental illness.
Alibi:

If a woman comes home pregnant or with a sexually transmitted disease after having an affair she can transform her position from adulteress to victim with just three words, *"I was raped."*

If a woman wants to swap her boring husband for her more interesting lover she may feel she needs to justify her actions to her friends, family and children who will probably condemn her for her act of betrayal but if she claims marital rape or violence she will gain the support of everyone. Her boring husband will be ostracised and her lover will become her knight in shining armor rescuing his damsel in distress.

If a woman commits an act of violence she can justify it in court by claiming to have been raped. When Lorena Bobbit was arrested for cutting off her husband's penis she told police it was punishment for him being a selfish lover but when it went to court she then said, *"I was raped."*

Rhiannon Brooker faked rape claims as an excuse for failing her law exams.

Brooker was convicted at Bristol Crown Court of perverting the course of justice after she claimed her then boyfriend had beaten her, forced her to have sex and also caused her to miscarry. She also faked injuries to suggest he hit her.

Source:

http://www.bbc.com/news/uk-england-bristol-28045679

Revenge:

A false rape claim is a formidable weapon that a weaker person can use to attack a much stronger person.

If a jilted woman or a man wants to hurt an ex lover they can easily do so with just a word, with the added bonus that when he goes to prison he will be separated from any new lover.

When I was 14, a male teacher angered one of his pupils. A plot was then hatched to accuse this teacher of raping one of the boys in the stationary cupboard. The anger subsided and the plan was never acted upon but it very nearly was and if it had been it would have probably ended the teacher's career, his marriage and possibly even his life. All too often the falsely accused see the only way out as suicide.

Attention Seeking:

Attention seeking comes in many forms, self-harm, Munchhausen syndrome, Munchhausen syndrome by proxy, false confessions and false allegations etc. Some false rape claims are just one example of attention seeking behaviour. These are often characterised by many accusations against multiple victims.

Regret:

If someone is told all their life that sex is dirty and wrong or they wake up next to the wrong person or someone of the wrong gender after they got carried away with the moment and things went further than they had intended it may be more acceptable in their own mind to reclassify persuasion as coercion and enough alcohol to lower inhibitions as enough to void consent.

Doing something you didn't intend to do is a mistake not rape. Having sex without your consent is rape.

Regret-sex may evolve into a rape allegation when someone confides in a friend who tells them, *"If you didn't want to then it's rape."* If in the cold light of day you regret your consent you can't retrospectively withdraw that consent.

For some, sex brings with it guilt and shame. It is normal human behaviour to transfer guilt to some degree, that's why it's so necessary to hear both sides of every story, if you then add in pressure from peers and parents who refuse to believe that a good religious girl would have done such a thing if she were not forced into it and the encouragement of the police who desperately want to see this man safely behind bars, it then becomes more and more difficult for the accuser to say, *"well actually, perhaps it wasn't as bad as all that."*

Money:

In recent years there has been a spate of high profile celebrities accused of rape or sexual assault. Many of these accusations have been found to be true but others were completely disproved, Cliff Richard, Jimmy Tarbuck, Paul Gambaccini, Jim Davidson...

The problem is proving who is a genuine victim and who has jumped on the bandwagon in the hope of fame or fortune.

One of Cliff Richard's accusers also tried to blackmail him. Given the damage done by even a clearly false allegation, I wonder how many rich, famous, or ordinary people have quietly paid up.

Source:
http://www.independent.co.uk/news/uk/crime/cliff-richard-sex-abuse-blackmail-police-rape-a7089896.html

Empowerment:

An accusation of rape is a game changer. In a divorce or if a custardy battle is not going your way then an accusation of rape will instantly give you the moral high ground and greatly increase your chances of winning.

Children may also be removed from the accused until the truth can be established and once this has happened the chance of the children's lives being disrupted again to return them to the accused is very small.

Mental illness:

FALSE RAPE CLAIMS

Many years ago I worked with a man who was accused of rape. He was questioned over several days then told by the police that they believed no rape had occurred.

The accuser's mother also worked with us and when the accusation was made she took the accused colleague to one side and said, *"This won't affect us working together, I don't think you did anything. I don't know why but she says this about all her boyfriends."*

The police knew this woman and knew her history so were skeptical from the start but this would not have been the case for the first man she accused.

A Sheffield crown court took just 45 minutes to clear a man of rape after he had been driven to the verge of suicide. Some of the jury members then broke down in tears when the judge told them that in a previous rape allegation that never went to court because it lacked credibility, the accused man actually did take his own life.

Source:
http://www.dailymail.co.uk/news/article-1280926/Student-cleared-rape-emerges-second-man-committed-suicide-falsely-accused-woman.html

Rape is so common that there are inevitably women and men who have been raped on different occasions by different rapists. Multiple accusations do not necessarily mean any of them are false. A woman who makes a dozen false rape accusations may also become a target for a real rapist, after all who would believe her?

On the other side of the coin, 'victim' anonymity means that if one man is falsely accused and goes to prison, he will never know about the dozen other men who were accused and cleared in similar circumstances.

In the case of Jemma Beale who falsely accused 15 men of rape (a crime for which she was jailed for 10 years) it was only because an ex-girlfriend of Beale's alerted police to the false rape accusations that an innocent man was released from prison after serving almost 3 years.

Source:
http://news.sky.com/story/very-convincing-liar-jemma-beale-jailed-for-false-rape-claims-11003341

Someone who makes multiple rape claims is either a fantasist or unfortunate. No decision can be made as to which without a full investigation that considers both possibilities.

Solidarity:

Naming the accused in a rape case means other victims have a chance to come forward which considerably strengthens the prosecutions case, however there is also the possibility that a friend or even a stranger who doesn't want to see another rapist get away with it, may make a false accusation.

Character assignation:

In modern politics accusations of sexual misconduct have become normal. No smear campaign is complete without a sex scandal of some sort. It's not necessary to provide any evidence. It's enough to simply ask the question, *"Is the candidate a rapist or better still a pedophile?"* on social media.

If you throw enough mud some will stick.

Mistakes:

The innocence project proves beyond any doubt that even after due process mistakes are still made.

Identity is known in 90% of rape cases but in the other 10% we need to find the rapist. To do this we usually rely on the victim giving us an account of what happened and a description of the attacker but our memory is nowhere near as reliable as we think it is.

We forget things. We wrongly think that we remember far more than we do because we don't remember how much we have forgotten.

Source:
http://www.newyorker.com/science/maria-konnikova/idea-happened-memory-recollection

We remember things differently, no two accounts of the same event are ever the same.

False memories can be inadvertently given to a witness for example...

If a police officer asks a witness *"Did the man have a snake tattoo?"* The witness will try the image of the tattoo against their recollection of the man and even if they are not sure about what they saw every time they are asked to think about it, the image of the tattoo will be reinforced in their memory until they are quite certain the man they saw had a snake tattoo.

If the police asked about the tattoo because a man of about the same height with a tattoo was seen on CCTV at about the same time then a vague description becomes a positive identification.

In 1975 an Australian psychologist, Donald Thomson, went to a television studio to discuss the psychology of eyewitness testimony. At the very moment he was discussing how people could best remember the faces of criminals, there was someone encoding Thomson's face as a rapist.

The day after the television broadcast Thomson was picked up by local police. He was told that last night a woman was raped and left unconscious in her apartment. She had named Thomson as her attacker.

Thomson was shocked, but had a watertight alibi. He had been on television at the time of the attack and in the

presence of the assistant commissioner of police.
It seemed that the victim had been watching Thomson on television just prior to being attacked. She had then confused his face with that of her attacker.

What would have been the outcome if the interview had been recorded and Thomson didn't have an alibi?

Source:
http://www.spring.org.uk/2008/02/how-memories-are-distorted-and-invented.php

An unknowable number of rapes are never reported. Of the rape accusations that are reported most are true but what is also true is that among the rapes that are reported there are a significant number of false rape claims.

The promise that victims will be believed inevitably means that the alleged perpetrator will not be believed. This presumption of guilt is the reverse of the accepted position in all other crimes.

In a rape case there are three possible outcomes. The rapist was found guilty and duly punished, the rape was found to be a false allegation and probably re-classified as no crime, or there is insufficient evidence to know for sure either way.

Rape is a serious crime with serious consequences for the victim that must be thoroughly investigated.

A false accusation of rape is a serious crime with serious

consequences for the victim (the accused) that must also be thoroughly investigated.

Women and men who report rape should keep their life long anonymity to encourage victims to come forward and reduce further emotional damage even though this may prevent the accused finding out that she or he is a serial accuser.

Given that a false rape allegation can cost the accused his reputation, his marriage, his house, his career, his mental health, a great deal of money and even his life, it is right that the accused should also have anonymity at least until there is enough evidence to bring charges, even though this may prevent the police finding out she or he is not the accused's first victim.

The identity of the accuser and the accused should be hidden from the public but not the police. The police need to be able to see if the accuser has made other accusations and if they were found to be credible and they need to be able to see if there have been other accusations made about the accused.

Women dominated juries are less likely to convict in a rape trial. If men and women come to a different conclusion when presented with the same evidence one of them is clearly wrong.

Source:
http://www.irishexaminer.com/ireland/stanford-rape-case-female-dominated-juries-less-likely-to-convict-in-rape-cases-404525.html

We already have specialist teams who deal with rapes in police stations but we should also have specialist teams to prosecute rape cases, with specialist jurors who know that rape victims react differently and not always in the way you would expect. Jurors must also know that although most rape accusations are genuine some are not and in those cases the victim is the accused person not the accuser.

If a false rape accusation is malicious and made for revenge, alibi, money etc, then the accuser should face prosecution with a penalty appropriate for the level of damage they inflicted on their victim (the accused) but if the false accusation was because of a personality disorder or mental illness then they need treatment not punishment but the police must also be able to access a database telling them who is likely to make false accusations in order to protect the innocent.

EQUALITY FOR WOMEN IS AN OXYMORON

Chapter 11

Domestic violence

EQUALITY FOR WOMEN IS AN OXYMORON

Domestic violence

> *"We may never be strong enough to be entirely non-violent in thought, word and deed, but we must keep non-violence as our goal and make strong progress towards it."*
>
> GHANDI

Domestic violence is the main reason I felt I had to write this book. I truly believe that by looking at domestic violence from a different angle we can greatly reduce it.

To solve any social problem we must first understand what is happening. We all know the stereotype of the drunken man who comes home from the pub to his terrified wife, who he then proceeds to beat to within an inch of her life or further.

These men exist and they are certainly part of the problem but there is another and I believe more common scenario that leads to more injuries and deaths and understanding this could potentially save many lives.

It was a radio broadcast in which Erin Pizzey, (the woman that opened and ran the first woman's refuge) suggested that women are as violent as men that changed my whole view on domestic violence.

In domestic violence there are victims and perpetrators,

winners and losers but it's a mistake to start with the premise that we can determine which is which by looking at their gender rather than their actions.

When people fight, the instigator is not always the winner and the victim is not always the looser.

FACT:

In 40% of domestic violence calls to the police, it's the man that is the victim.

This will surprise many, I was certainly surprised when I read this, so I cross-checked it by looking at the statistics in the USA and Australia and found they have similar numbers.

Source:
http://www.theguardian.com/society/2010/sep/05/men-victims-domestic-violence

FACT:

Men make up almost 1 in 5 of the victims killed by their partners.

In 2014/15 there were 81 women and 19 men who were killed by their partner.

Source:
http://www.telegraph.co.uk/men/thinking-man/why-female-violence-against-men-is-societys-last-great-taboo/

DOMESTIC VIOLENCE

In a "fair fight" to the death between a man and a woman, what odds do you think you would get on the woman winning?

I doubt if you could get a bookmaker to give you better than a hundred to one against but the actual number of deaths by gender is four women to one man, this is because men often hold back, still applying the "men don't hit women rule" and because women more commonly use a weapon of some sort to even up the odds a bit.

We know that most domestic violence against women is never reported to the police. I believe that because of the added humiliation of having to admit that he has been beaten-up by his wife, domestic violence against men is even less likely to be reported.

The statistics suggest that Erin Pizzey is right and that violence against men is at least as common as violence against women and for the sake of both genders we need to make it as socially unacceptable for a woman to hit a man as it is for a man to hit a woman. This will benefit both men and women because if a woman changes an argument into a fight by using physical violence against a man she is much more likely to get a physical response with possibly fatal consequences.

Boys learn from a very early age that if you hit someone who is bigger and stronger than you are, then you will probably get hurt, they also learn it is not acceptable to hit girls. This does not always stop them doing so of course, but they do know that it's wrong.

It is my belief that if we can make violence against men as unacceptable as violence against women then we will reduce the number of women who are then hurt or killed by men either in self-defence or retaliation!

Why are men airbrushed out?

In the murder statistics, we don't discriminate by colour, all the victims are counted irrespective of their race, neither do we discriminate by religion, all religions are included in the statistics, so why are men not included in most of the statistics quoted for domestic violence?

In society and in the media violence against women is virtually always (and quite rightly) seen as unacceptable.

In films and whodunits we see a lot of violence against women with the rest of the plot mostly concerned with finding and punishing the baddies who have committed this heinous crime.

Men can also be the dead body in the murder to be solved but they are all too often portrayed as just collateral damage. The expendable soldier or security men shot or blown up. We do not engage with these men, they have no back-story, they live for an instant on the screen and are never thought of again.

DOMESTIC VIOLENCE

This is mostly violence against men by men but when it's violence against men by women in the media and on TV it's often treated as either, not serious, acceptable or worst of all funny.

This constant portrayal of violence against men as OK, not only has a negative affect on men but also negative and sometimes fatal affect on women.

Let me give you some examples of violence by women against men on TV being accepted, ignored or laughed at...

Over the few weeks that it took to write this section, on the BBC soap EastEnders we saw three attacks on men by women.

In one episode we saw an attack on the character Fatboy treated in a light-hearted way.

Fatboy was annoying Shirley, a feisty character who grabbed him between the legs and said, *"Do I need to squeeze really hard?"* Fatboy limps back to his friend and says something like *"That woman is really scary."*

At around the same time Fatboy serenades Leon's would-be girlfriend Zsa Zsa from a DJ van. When Zsa Zsa has had enough of this she comes out of her house with a baseball bat and beats Fatboy round the legs with it. The scriptwriters treated this as if a baseball bat were a perfectly reasonable way to deal with an unwanted serenade.

Source:
https://www.youtube.com/watch?v=nRwzMbAbcdQ
https://www.youtube.com/watch?v=iEAM8Ixrnxo

A few weeks later the scriptwriters pushed the boundaries even further by having the character Libby, slap the face of her wheelchair bound boyfriend Adam. This act was actually greeted by applause from a group of other characters! I wonder if they would have been shown clapping if the genders were reversed, with a man hitting his disabled girlfriend and I wonder how many complaints they would have received?

Source:
https://www.youtube.com/watch?v=uMcOMl2kcCE

Yes, I know EastEnders is not real and the scriptwriters would have a pretty boring program if they didn't spice things up a bit but the constant portrayal of female violence against men as acceptable, leads some people to think it really is OK or even normal for women to hit men and that they can do so with impunity.

When we look at violence used as humour we can't leave out the seaside postcard.

DOMESTIC VIOLENCE

EQUALITY FOR WOMEN IS AN OXYMORON

We have all seen the postcards of the scrawny man coming home late from the pub, bottle in hand with a bemused look on his face, unaware of the fate that awaits him, but we can see his brawny wife hiding behind the door with a face like thunder, rolling pin or frying pan at the ready.

It is quite easy to kill someone with either of these weapons but we still see the funny side of it.

If you are still not convinced that violence against men is not taken seriously then simply reverse the roles. Do we still find these postcards funny when the genders are swapped?

Imagine the same postcard with a petite woman leaving a nightclub after a girly night out, glass in hand, hair all askew with her bruiser of a husband waiting for her and taking his belt off!

Still funny? If not, why not?

DOMESTIC VIOLENCE

Is domestic violence against men ignored?

Was Tiger Woods a battered husband?

What comes to mind when you think about Tiger Woods? I didn't deliberately follow the case but the massive coverage given to Tiger Woods' affairs and his subsequent marital problems were impossible to avoid, yet in all the media frenzy I didn't hear one word about the attack by Mrs Woods on her husband.

We weren't there and can never be absolutely certain as to what happened but if we look at the evidence as portrayed by the media it looks almost certain that Tiger Woods was a victim of domestic violence...

The story broke with the revelation that Tiger Woods had had several affairs. There followed news reports that the police had been called to a domestic incident and that Tiger Woods had had two minor car crashes one into a tree and one into a fire hydrant. His wife then smashed the back window of the car with a golf club and it all ended with Tiger Woods being taken to hospital with what the police described as *"injuries not consistent with a road traffic accident."*

These events were explained like this...

There was a row after Mrs Woods found out about her husband's affairs. Mr Woods leaves but has two car accidents outside the house. His wife seeing the man she loves in danger puts the row to one side and tries to rescue her husband by breaking the back window and dragging him to safety. There is no mention made of the *"injuries not consistent with a road traffic accident."*

In the heat of an emergency, untrained people don't always work in the most effective way but even if we assume all the doors had been jammed shut in the minor impact, to attempt to drag a man with unknown injuries over the back of the front seats, then over the back seats, then through the broken back window doesn't seem likely to have been the best course of action.

Is this not a much more likely scenario?

Mrs Woods confronts her husband over his affairs. In the row that ensues Mrs Woods inflicts the *"injuries not consistent with a road traffic accident."*

These injuries are not described, but if they are not consistent with a road traffic accident then I am thinking something like claw marks down the face, a hand shaped bruise or maybe a lump with the words "Five iron" picked out in bruising.

Mr Woods now has the choice - fight or flight. He chooses flight and tries to make his getaway but his wife has not finished with him yet and tries to head off the car wielding a golf cub causing the accidents, then in her anger Mrs

DOMESTIC VIOLENCE

Woods does a *'Basil Faulty'* on the car with the golf club smashing the back window. The police then arrive saving Mr Woods from further injury.

In this version of events Mr Woods was attacked by his wife but despite being a super fit professional sportsman and a good deal stronger than his wife he did not fight back but chose to try and leave. (At this point the feminists should be holding Tiger Woods up as a role model. Despite his previous indiscretions, his non-violent response to a violent attack is surely worthy of the highest praise.)

When the police arrived he then defended his wife claiming the attack was a rescue attempt. (We often see this response in women who constantly walk into doors leaving hand shaped bruises.)

This to me is almost certainly a case of violence against a man being ignored by the media who were so very very interested in this case yet don't seem to have noticed this side of it at all.

How do you think it would have played out in the media, if Mr Woods had come home to find his wife had been having the affairs, if he had put her in hospital, if he had chased her out of the house with a golf club?

Would the affairs justify the attack and would it be Mrs Woods making the public apology?

EQUALITY FOR WOMEN IS AN OXYMORON

In June 1993, 24 year old Lorena Bobbit cut off her husband's penis while he slept. She claimed in court that he had raped her, however when first arrested she told police it was because, *"He always has orgasm and he doesn't wait for me to have orgasm."* *"He's selfish. I don't think it's fair, so I pulled back the sheets then and I did it."*

Source:
http://www.nytimes.com/1994/01/22/us/lorena-bobbitt-acquitted-in-mutilation-of-husband.html?pagewanted=all

If Lorena Bobbit cut off her husband's penis as a punishment for being a selfish lover what could she have possibly used as her defence in court?

Bear in mind that even a self-defence argument doesn't work in the Bobbit case. Killing a man will stop him hurting you again, but cutting off his penis can really only be classed as revenge.

There are of course two sides to every story and John Bobbit had just been acquitted a few months earlier for marital rape (which begs the question why were they still together). He was also arrested on several occasions after their inevitable divorce for various assaults on subsequent partners.

This case ended when they both went to court, he was accused of sexual assault and she was accused of malicious wounding they were both acquitted, her on the grounds of insanity.

DOMESTIC VIOLENCE

John Bobbit was arrested for various assaults on women both before and after this case and his now ex-wife was arrested in 1988 for punching her mother.

It seems this couple were both violent.

The act of cutting off a man's penis is more common than you might think...

In one case in 2011, a 50 year old California woman, Catherine Kieu, was found guilty of torture and aggravated mayhem after cutting off her husband's penis and then putting it into the waste disposal, she was given a sentence of seven years to life in state prison.

Prosecutors argued that Kieu refused to accept her husband's demand for a divorce and carried out the attack as part of a revenge plot.

Kieu drugged her husband's tofu with sleeping pills, tied him to his bed then screamed out 3 times, *"You deserve it, you deserve it, you deserve it"*! Before attacking him with a 10-inch kitchen knife and the whole thing was captured by a voice-activated recorder that Kieu had hidden in the bedroom.

This case was the subject discussed on 'The Talk', a TV show in which five women sat round a table laughing hysterically about a man having his penis cut off.

During this program Sharon Osbourne actually said, *"I do think it's quite fabulous."* and *"Can you imagine that thing whizzing around in the waste disposal, it's hysterical."* She said this knowing the victim was still in hospital but not knowing his crime was simply to ask for a divorce.

Most sickening of all is not a few sick women laughing at male genital mutilation but that the live audience of women also found it so very funny.

Source:
https://www.youtube.com/watch?v=kkmanLIAdXI

Kieu's actions may, in a small part be explained by the fact that she was from Vietnam, a country where women cut off their men's penises often enough for it to have been given it's own name, it's called, *"feeding the ducks"* because the women normally throw the penis into a river or lake.

If after cutting off a man's penis, you then throw it into a field as in the Bobbit case or throw it into a river as in feeding the ducks or put it into a waste disposal unit, then the intention is the same, to prevent any attempt to re-attach it.

Despite the vicious, cold, calculating nature of these cases, when it goes to court the defence is normally one of self-defence because self-defence is one of the very few legitimate reasons for violence against another, regardless of gender.

DOMESTIC VIOLENCE

Source:
https://www.theguardian.com/education/2012/nov/19/improbable-research-thai-women-cut-off-penis

Domestic violence, hurts, injures and kills but unfortunately violence is also part of our normal behaviour but that does not mean violence is inevitable or acceptable. We can choose not to hit each other.

There is no doubt that some women can be extremely violent as can some men but this is not about blame it's about outcomes! Putting aside the rights and wrongs of individual cases, the stark fact remains that if a woman makes a physical attack on a man she is very likely to get a physical response.

I am not trying to excuse male violence or even shift the blame a bit, all I am calling for is a 'No First Strike' policy.

If we start with the premise that violence particularly against someone weaker than you is wrong and that violence against someone stronger than you is wrong and stupid we are almost there. Surely everyone, even the most extreme *"Castrate them at birth"* feminazi can see the sense in *"No first strike."*

A 'No First Strike' policy will reduce the amount of violence but it will not end it completely so there must always be somewhere safe women and men can run to.

At the time of writing there were 7,500 refuges for women

and only 60 for men. If men and women are indeed equally at risk of attack, then despite their superior physical strength, having less than 1% of refuges for men is not enough.

If we look at violence as a whole most victims of violence are men.

If women had parity with men, their murder rate would double.

If we look at violence as a whole most perpetrators are also men.

It is only when we separate out domestic violence between men and women that the balance changes.

This requires much more analysis but what appears to be happening is this…

Men are more violent but the violence is mostly directed against men.

Women are less violent with their violence also mostly directed against men.

The statistics suggest that either through nature or nurture or probably some of each, the reluctance of men to hit women (relative to men hitting men) balances their higher aggression and the social acceptance of women hitting men balances their lower level of overall violence with the result

DOMESTIC VIOLENCE

that in domestic violence men hit women and women hit men in about equal proportions.

Women are still 4 times more likely to die in domestic violence than men but this is for physiological reasons. Women are smaller, weaker and more fragile so in a fight, the level of physical damage is much higher for women.

Men are bigger and stronger so can do more damage and their extra muscle also protects against injury. Men also have bigger brains than women but this difference is mostly made up of things like gristle so this does not mean men are more intelligent, just harder to kill.

If we could extend the 'boys don't hit girls' effect to include 'girls don't hit boys', then I think we could reduce the number of attacks significantly and we would also prevent countless injuries and save quite a few relationships and as if that were not enough we would also save millions of pounds.

The cost of treating the physical health of victims of domestic violence, (including hospital, GP, ambulance, prescriptions) is put at 23 billion pounds.

Source:
http://news.bbc.co.uk/2/hi/uk_news/3616542.stm

With the cure costing so much perhaps we should look at spending a bit more on prevention.

EQUALITY FOR WOMEN IS AN OXYMORON

Chapter 12

Erin Pizzey

EQUALITY FOR WOMEN IS AN OXYMORON

Erin Pizzey

"If we have any hope of tackling the tragic effects of domestic violence we have to face the facts that women can and are also guilty of violence against their partners.

To concentrate only on women as victims is to deny the fact that children are also abused by their mothers. We can no longer afford to cover up the huge scandal that has existed for the last forty years where only men have been held up as perpetrators of all violence."

ERIN PIZZEY

The first internationally recognised refuge for battered women was opened in 1971 by Erin Pizzey.

The effect of having domestic violence brought out of the shadows and thrust into the spotlight meant that every one pulled together to fill the gaping hole in our social care system.

Citing the parable of the good Samaritan the local vicar instructed his flock to donate children's toys or grown out of clothes to the refuge and to do whatever else they could to help.

The DHSS classified the women as homeless and the refuges as rented accommodation so paid the rent in the form of housing benefit added to the women's other benefits, ensuring they had all the houses they needed to keep going and the feminists gave Erin Pizzey the moral support and the volunteers she needed to continue her pioneering project.

This is what should have happened but what actually happened was none of the above…

The church branded her a marriage wrecker, the DHSS said the women had homes to go to and were not eligible for any benefits at all and the feminists turned on Erin Pizzey because she would not follow the feminist agenda of demonising all men.

In her book 'Prone to Violence' Pizzey says, "*I never saw Women's Aid as a movement that was hostile to men, but The National Federation, which quickly formed, made it quite clear that men were the enemy.*"

Pizzey wrote that much domestic violence was reciprocal with both partners abusing each other in roughly equal measure. She reached this conclusion when she asked the women in her refuge about their violence, only to discover most of the women were equally as violent or more violent than their husbands.

In her study "Comparative Study of Battered Women And Violence-Prone Women," (co-researched with Dr. John Gayford of Warlingham Hospital), Pizzey distinguishes between 'genuine battered women' and 'violence-prone women' the former defined as "*the unwilling and innocent *victim of his or her partner's violence"* and the latter defined as *"the unwilling victim of his or her own violence."* This study reports that 62% of the sample population were more accurately described as 'violence prone.' Similar findings regarding the mutuality of domestic violence have been confirmed in subsequent studies.

Source:
http://web.csulb.edu/~mfiebert/assault.htm
http://www.dewar4research.org/DOCS/dky.pdf

Erin Pizzey's book led to outrage from the extreme feminists.

Describing the harassment directed at Erin Pizzey, Deborah Ross of The Independent wrote that, "*The feminist sisterhood went bonkers*" and Pizzey had to be given police protection.

At the promotional events for Erin Pizzey's books, she was confronted with banners that read "*All men are rapists*" and "*All men are bastards.*"

Pizzey and her family received death and bomb threats and after she was told that all her post had to be checked by the bomb squad, Pizzey decided to leave the country.

At about the same time in the USA Suzanne Steinmetz was saying the same sort of things and got much the same treatment.

According to ifeminist.com, the fem-thugs began by telephoning the University of Delaware's faculty members, deriding Steinmetz's work as "*anti-feminist*." Then they leveled threats against Steinmetz and her children. Sponsors of her speaking engagements started to receive threatening phone calls. Finally, a bomb threat was called into a meeting where Steinmetz was scheduled to speak.

Source:
http://www.ifeminists.net/introduction/editorials/2005/0525roberts.html

These examples of feminist attacks on Pizzey and Steinmetz took place a long time ago but if we look at the protests against Warren Farrell in 2012 we see that not much has changed.

At the University of Toronto, people who wanted to see Warren Farrell were faced with chants of *"Fuck Warren Farrell, Fuck Warren Farrell, Fuck Warren Farrell!"* and *"All men's rights groups are hate groups."*

The irony of holding up banners reading *"All men's rights groups are hate groups"* whilst screaming *"Fuck Warren Farrell, Fuck Warren Farrell"* at the top of their voices seems to have been lost on the protesters.

The feminists both male and female stopped people from getting in to hear what Farrell had to say. The position of the extreme feminists seems to be - Agree with us or face the consequences!

Source:
https://www.youtube.com/watch?v=iARHCxAMAO0

Some men's rights groups at the extreme end, could indeed be described as misogynistic hate groups. Some extreme feminist groups are most definitely misandric hate groups. How would the feminists react if some of the more hateful slogans of the women's movement were applied to them?

What if *"All men are bastards, pigs, scum, rapists, pedophiles"* read *"All women are bitches"* etc etc, or...

What if *"A woman needs a man, like a fish needs a bicycle"*, read *"A man needs a woman like a fish needs a bicycle."*

"Castrate them at birth"...

"Men have only two faults everything they say and everything they do"...

Mugs with the words *"Men's tears"* printed on them.

These frequently heard chants are not anti-discrimination they are clearly anti-men and as such can only accurately be described as misandry.

If we look at domestic violence between mothers and children the size and strength advantage now lies with the woman and a fact that surprises most people is that in domestic murders where the victim is a child the murder is almost as likely to be committed by the mother as by the biological father.

Source:
http://www.dewar4research.org/docs/chom.pdf

Note: Statistics on filicide often include previous partners, subsequent partners, stepfathers and biological fathers as parents so the list of suspects may be 1 woman (the mother) and several men as the fathers even if they are not biologically related to the victim.

Which gender kills most children in the UK depends on what you count...

Children killed by strangers:

Children killed by strangers are almost always killed by men but are very rare with 3 cases being recorded in 2015.

Children killed by parents (biological and non-biological):

Children killed by biological and non-biological parents are almost twice as likely to be killed by men.

Children killed by biological parents:

The number of children killed by their biological mother is about equal to the number killed by their biological father.

Children killed at birth:

Children killed at birth are almost always killed by their mother. The numbers of neonaticides are unclear because they are almost certainly under reported on death certificates and an unknown number of pregnancies are kept hidden.

Every year we hear of a newborn baby being found dead in a rubbish sack and an appeal then goes out for the mother to come forward. The women who commit neonaticide usually conceal the pregnancy, kill the baby then hide the body. It is highly probable that there are many more babies killed in this way each year that are not known about. Nobody will miss a baby they never knew existed and it's not hard to hide such a small body.

Children killed legally:

Mothers who smoke during pregnancy damage their unborn children with over 300 a year dying, that's almost 1 a day. If you include miscarriages caused by smoking then the number goes up to 5,000 a year, that's 13 a day.

Abortion:

There were 185,000 abortions carried out in 2014, that's 500 a day. I am not against early abortion and the vast majority of the UK abortions are very early.

Prenatal and in the first year of life, a child is far more likely to be killed by their mother. Older children are more likely to be killed by their father or another man.

The point I am trying to make here is that the premise that men are always a danger and women are never a danger to children is false. The statistics show that children from broken homes (almost always living with their mother) are at greater risk of violence and the feminist assertion that, *"Marriage is not a safe place for women and children"* actually puts children at risk.

The safest place for a child is not with mum or with dad but with both.

The risk to a child in a family where the parents have separated is far higher than if the parents are together and few child murders occur without some warning, so good contact with both biological parents acts as a protection for the child.

Source:

http://www.christian.org.uk/news/children-from-broken-homes-at-high-risk-of-abuse/

https://www.theguardian.com/world/2016/may/17/abortion-rate-england-and-wales-five-year-high

http://www.mirror.co.uk/lifestyle/health/300-babies-die-every-year-2005115

http://www.bbc.com/news/world-europe-11951091

https://karenwoodall.wordpress.com/2013/10/04/gender-biased-family-services-killing-children-in-the-uk/

https://www.ons.gov.uk/peoplepopulationandcommunity/crimeandjustice/compendium/focusonviolentcrimeandsexualoffences/yearendingmarch2015/chapter2homicide#relationship-between-victim-and-principal-suspect

Some men kill their children and some men kill their wives this does not justify demonising all men any more than it justifies demonising all women because some women kill their children or their husbands.

Violence against a man and violence against a woman is equally wrong but it is not the same. Violence against women is more serious because women are more easily damaged and violence against children is most serious of all, for the same reason. Men are also normally bigger and stronger than women, which must reduce their level of fear when being attacked but this is not about blame it's about outcomes.

If we want to reduce the level of violence (and I think we can), then we must not just aim at the right target but aim at all the targets! We must condemn people for their actions not just their gender.

Extreme Feminism is operated much like a religion, there can be no descent and no questioning of the official line. Anyone who dares to suggest that men are anything less than the Devil's spawn is guilty of blasphemy or misogyny and must be silenced or punished.

Feminism is about justice, fairness and ideology at it's roots but like many religions, at the top it's all about power, manipulation and money. It's no surprise to me that Emmeline Pankhurst went from preaching feminism to preaching religion.

EQUALITY FOR WOMEN IS AN OXYMORON

Chapter 13

The Suffragettes - Heroines or terrorists?

EQUALITY FOR WOMEN IS AN OXYMORON

The Suffragettes - Heroines or terrorists?

"When you have warfare, things happen; people suffer; the noncombatants suffer as well as the combatants. And so it happens in civil war."

EMMELINE PANKHURST

Ask almost anyone about the Suffragettes and they will tell you how men had the vote but women did not and how Emmeline Pankhurst and her daughter Christabel along with others were brutally treated simply for saying women should be allowed to vote.

If this were true, the Suffragettes are clearly heroines but if we look past this airbrushed version of women's suffrage then history paints quite a different picture.

FACT:

There has never been a time in British history when all men had the vote and all women did not.

There were times when a few rich men had the vote and women did not.

There were also times when all men had the vote but some women did not because the voting age for men and women was not equal.

As things stand now, men and women have voting parity but not full suffrage of course.

We still have an unelected religious leader as head of state and we still have an unelected second chamber also filled with religious leaders and the bit we do get to elect is so dominated by money and privilege that the only real choice is which millionaire public schoolboy is least likely to widen the gap between the working class and the ruling class!

So would you support a Suffragette style campaign of violence, to finish the job and fight to give the UK its first real democracy?

It's quite clear from the quote at the beginning of this chapter that Emmeline Pankhurst considered the fight for votes to be a civil war and one in which it was acceptable for the non-combatants to suffer.

For a war you need an army and the best way to raise an army is to tell the people that the enemy is at the gate and create a feeling of us and them.

For Emmeline and Christabel Pankhurst, the chosen enemy was men and despite working class men not having the vote either, they were never included in the fight for suffrage.

Despite many men supporting women's suffrage the Pankhursts chose to make the fight men vs women rather than suffrage for all.

THE SUFFRAGETTES - HEROINES OR TERRORISTS?

The struggle for a few privileged women to get parity with a few privileged men was not likely to get mass support but by dressing it up as women against men rather than rich against poor, the Suffragette propaganda machine was able to call all the sisters to arms.

The Pankhursts presented their war as a fight for justice and equality but in reality the Pankhursts were...

Against votes for working-class women;

Against votes for working-class men;

Against votes for the women in their own organisation.

Far from wanting to end the inequality of votes only for the privileged few, the Pankhursts actually fought to keep it;

At the top of the organization, the Suffragettes didn't want to end the divide between the haves and the have-nots they just wanted to put privileged women like themselves on the "haves" side of the divide, with no votes for the working class of either gender.

FACT:

Emmeline and Christabel Pankhurst fought **against** universal suffrage.

Source:
hotdog://spartacus-educational.coma/Workups.host

EQUALITY FOR WOMEN IS AN OXYMORON

I wonder how many of the working class women that were recruited by the likes of ex-mill worker Annie Kenney, knew that 'Votes for women' should have actually read 'Votes for ladies' and that the vote was never intended for the likes of them?

There is a good argument to be made for not giving uneducated silly women the responsibility of making important decisions like who runs the country but by the end of the 19th century many men had realized that women are no sillier than men and people like John Stuart Mill were proposing votes for women and getting large numbers of the all male MPs to vote in favour of it.

The newly formed Labour Party was in favour of universal suffrage not the partial suffrage only for the rich advocated by the Pankhursts with Ada Nigel Chew, a leading woman in the Labour party saying that she rejected the policies of the Suffragettes in favour of... *"The abolition of all existing anomalies, which would enable a man or woman to vote simply because they are man or woman, not because they are more fortunate financially than their fellow men and women"*.

How ironic, the thing preventing the Suffragettes from becoming allied with the new Labour party, which was destined to become the government, was their refusal to accept universal suffrage.

Our airbrushed version of history also makes much of the

THE SUFFRAGETTES - HEROINES OR TERRORISTS?

brutal treatment received by the Suffragettes but the vast majority of the violence in Mrs Pankhurst's war was at the hands of the Suffragettes.

There are thousands of recorded incidents of violent acts conducted by the Suffragettes, here are just a few...

Assaults:

On the evening of 13 October 1905, Christabel Pankhurst and Annie Kenney disrupted a meeting of the Liberal party at the Free Trade Hall by shouting *"Will the Liberal Government give women the vote?"* An uproar ensued, as Liberal stewards and plain-clothes police tried to remove the women from the hall and Christabel and Annie struggled against their ejection. (Up to this point I am in support of the women's protest.)

According to testimony given the following day by Inspector Mather, the pair were informed they were in the presence of police officers and that they were free to leave but Christabel spat in the face of Superintendent Watson and then spat in Inspector Mather's face and struck him in the mouth, **saying that she wanted to assault a policeman**.

The women were then ejected into South Street, where, according to Mather, Christabel again struck him in the mouth. Christabel and Annie were charged with disorderly behaviour and obstructing a footway by causing a crowd to assemble. In addition, Christabel was charged with striking

Inspector Mather twice and with spitting at Mather and Watson.

On 3 June 1909, an irate feminist felled the editor of the Belfast Evening Telegraph with an unexpected blow, she was expelled from his office but then went on to the office of the editor of the Belfast Newsletter and struck him too. (He had angered her by urging those who found Suffragettes marring golf courses to take the law into their own hands.)

In London, on the same day as the Belfast assaults, two women used a dog whip to assault Dr Forward, the medical officer of Holloway Prison, where forced feeding was being carried out.

On 13 November 1909 Theresa Garnett, a member of the WSPU (The Women's Social and Political Union) was Charged with assaulting Winston Churchill with a whip, she said afterwards *"Has it hurt him much?"* Churchill was not hurt and did not press charges however Theresa Garnett was sent to prison for a month for disturbing the peace.

In another altercation Mrs Pankhurst lightly struck Inspector Jarvis in the face three times. He told her she was striking him for a purpose and that he would not be perturbed. After Mrs Pankhurst gave Inspector Jarvis two stronger blows and another woman knocked off his hat, arrests were obtained.

Assaulting police officers and politicians was a deliberate

THE SUFFRAGETTES - HEROINES OR TERRORISTS?

policy of the Suffragettes and by their own admission it was done with the intention of getting arrested. The Suffragettes were well aware of the propaganda value of newspaper reports and pictures of poor weak women being carried away by big burly policemen.

The Suffragettes formed a group of about 30 women called The Bodyguard who carried clubs and were trained in Jiu-Jitsu. These women were the Suffragette version of Special Forces.

The Jiu-Jitsu instructor Edith Garrud recalled in an interview in 1965, how a policeman once tried to prevent her from protesting outside Parliament. According to her account, the policeman said *"Now then, move on, you can't start causing an obstruction here,"*. *"Excuse me, it is you who are making an obstruction"*, she replied and threw him over her shoulder.

Source:
http://www.johndclare.net/Women1_SuffragetteActions_Rosen.htm

For most of these minor assaults the women would have either not been prosecuted or have been given a fine, they were only sent to prison when they refused to pay their fines or for much more serious offences.

Post box burning:

At the end of 1912, the Suffragettes launched simultaneous

attacks on post boxes across the entire country. The Suffragettes used acid or burning rags to set fire to the contents of hundreds of letter boxes damaging over 5,000 letters and postcards.

Telegraph cables cut:

In 1912 telephone and telegraph wires were cut with 23 trunk telegraph wires cut on the London Road at Potters Bar.

Window Breaking:

The Suffragettes began a nationwide campaign of smashing windows with Emmeline Pankhurst saying, *"The argument of the broken window pane is the most valuable argument in modern politics."*

On 29 June 1909, a group of thirteen women, using small stones wrapped in brown paper, began to break windows at the Privy Council, Treasury and Home Offices. To avoid injuring anyone, pieces of string had been tied to the stones, which were swung against the windows while held by the string and then dropped through the holes, again the window breakers were arrested immediately.

On the 1st of March 1912, around 150 women were standing in front of shop windows and government offices in London's West End, they then simultaneously took hammers and stones from their pockets and smashed the windows. The women didn't try to run away, it was a publicity stunt

THE SUFFRAGETTES - HEROINES OR TERRORISTS?

and again getting arrested was part of the plan.

Source:
http://www.bbc.com/news/magazine-16945901

In all, thousands of shop and office windows were smashed.

Sabotaging male sports venues:

The symbols of sole male preserves were attacked. Golf courses and bowling greens were dug up and huge slogans painted across the greens. Cricket pavilions were set alight, as were horse racing venues.

On 4 June 1913, Emily Wilding Davison travelled to Epsom Downs carrying two Suffragette flags, she squeezed through the railings and made an apparent grab for the reins of the King's horse. Davison was hit by the horse and suffered a fractured skull and internal bleeding, she died four days later in hospital.

There has been much controversy as to whether she intended to die or just pin a Suffragette flag to the King's horse. There was a return train ticket found in her pocket and she had booked a holiday with her sister suggesting she didn't mean to die, however she did also make other suicide attempts whilst in prison.

Source:
http://www.theguardian.com/world/2013/may/29/nine-lessons-Suffragettes-feminists

Art work destroyed:

On 4 May 1914, the Suffragette Mary Wood (an alias of Mary Aldham) attacked the Royal Academy's John Singer Sargent portrait of the author Henry James, breaking through the glass and slashing the canvas three times with a meat cleaver.

Wood wrote to the Women's Social and Political Union saying, "*I have tried to destroy a valuable picture because I wish to show the public that they have no security for their property nor for their art treasures until women are given the political freedom.*"

The Suffragettes also broke the protective glass of a number of paintings at Manchester Art Gallery and in 1914 Velazquez's famous Rokeby Venus was repeatedly slashed with a meat cleaver at the National Gallery.

Source:
https://www.royalacademy.org.uk/article/deeds-not-words-Suffragettes-and

Arson Attacks:

Across the country specially selected empty houses were burned down, many of them belonging to prominent members of society or as a personal attack on those who spoke out against the Suffragettes.

The Suffragettes burned down the refreshment rooms in

THE SUFFRAGETTES - HEROINES OR TERRORISTS?

several of the Royal Parks, they burned railway stations, a train, churches and much more.

Banners now started to appear reading, "Burning For The Vote!"

Source:
http://spartacus-educational.com/Warson.htm

Bombings:

The Suffragettes planted two bombs in an unfinished house being built for the Chancellor of the Exchequer, David Lloyd-George, one destroyed the servant's quarters the other was planted in the main house but failed to go off.

The British Museum had mummy cases damaged and a bomb was discovered in the Metropolitan Tabernacle.

A bomb went off under the dome at the Royal Astronomical Observatory on Blackford Hill, Edinburgh.

A bomb was placed beside the Coronation Chair in Westminster Abbey. It exploded causing slight damage to the chair and the 'Stone of Destiny' below it.

Several other bombs were planted including one in St Paul's Cathedral and one near the Bank of England.

Source:
http://www.historyhouse.co.uk/articles/Suffragettes.html

https://www.yooniqimages.com/images/detail/216304777/Editorial/Suffragette-arson-st-leonards

Attempted murder:

One of the most horrifying Suffragette attacks occurred in Dublin in 1912. Mary Leigh, Gladys Evans, Lizzie Baker and Mabel Capper attempted to set fire to the Theatre Royal during a packed lunchtime matinee attended by the Prime Minister Herbert Asquith. They left a canister of gunpowder close to the stage and hurled petrol and lit matches into the projection booth, which contained highly combustible film reels.

Earlier in the day, Mary Leigh had hurled a hatchet towards Asquith, which narrowly missed him and instead cut the Irish Nationalist MP John Redmond on the ear. Redmond's focus on the campaign for home rule had led to his refusal to insert a clause giving women the vote, assuring his status as a target.

Source:
http://www.historytoday.com/fern-riddell/weaker-sex-violence-and-suffragette-movement

There were also threats to shoot the Prime Minister Herbert Asquith.

A moderate Suffragette called Mrs Moor contacted the Metropolitan Police with a letter from a militant Suffragette containing the threat to shoot Asquith. Moore told officers

THE SUFFRAGETTES - HEROINES OR TERRORISTS?

she thought the situation was getting out of hand.

Source:
http://news.bbc.co.uk/2/hi/uk_news/5389984.stm

In an alleged incident took place in 1913 involving a magistrate, Sir Henry Curtis Bennett reveals how two Suffragettes tried to push him off a cliff. He was a target because he was one of the magistrates who had sentenced many of the Suffragettes.

Source:
http://query.nytimes.com/gst/abstract.html?res=9800E3D81F3AE633A25757C0A9609C946296D6CF&legacy=true

http://historyoffeminism.com/tag/suffragette-terrorism/

It was the stated aim of the Suffragettes not to kill anyone with Emmeline Pankhurst saying, *"Only human life is sacred."*

The Suffragettes didn't kill anyone but they would certainly have done so, if the First World War had not brought a truce between the government and the Suffragettes.

In the 8 years between 1906 and 1914 there were 1,214 court appearances, that's an average of 3 a week but they were not evenly spread over the 8 years. The number of attacks and the level of violence was rapidly escalating to the point where it was only luck that no innocent people had been killed.

Close Shaves:

The bomb and arson attack on the Theatre Royal while it was packed with people was obviously a close shave for both the audience and those working in the theatre.

When Emily Davison ran onto the racecourse to attach a Suffragette flag to the King's horse she was trampled and died in hospital a few days later. Emily Davison is now remembered as a martyr but it is only luck that the jockey and the horse (who both fell in the attack) were not also killed.

When the Suffragettes planted two bombs in a house that was under construction, one failed to go off, the other went off just 20 minutes before a dozen builders were due to start work.

The Suffragettes put lives at risk by making hoax fire calls.

The Suffragettes put lives at risk by cutting railway signal wires.

In Ilford, three streets had their fire alarm wires cut.

Source:
http://www.historytoday.com/fern-riddell/weaker-sex-violence-and-suffragette-movement#sthash.An5gqpGg.dpuf

Anyone reading this list of criminal acts committed by the Suffragettes will not be at all surprised that many of them

THE SUFFRAGETTES - HEROINES OR TERRORISTS?

were sent to prison. While in prison many of the Suffragettes went on hunger strike, demanding to be treated as political prisoners (which of course they were) rather than common criminals. This led to the force-feeding that we hear so much about.

I have seen force-feeding described as many things including 'rape' (which it clearly isn't) and the most commonly used word (the one chosen by the Suffragettes themselves) is 'torture' but force feeding isn't that either.

There is no doubt that holding someone down against their will, forcing their mouth open with a metal clamp then pushing a metre long tube into their stomach is a horrible experience but torture and force-feeding differ in two important ways.

The first difference is that the women were able to stop the force-feeding at any point.

Most of the women were not sent to prison but fined, they were only sent to prison when, as a protest they refused to pay their fines. When in prison the women were only force-fed because as a protest, they refused to eat.

The women went to prison to make a point and to force the hand of the government and their imprisonment and brutal treatment were a very important part of their propaganda war.

Emmeline Pankhurst's civil war was probably one of the first wars in which the main weapon was propaganda. A new form of warfare in which neither side could allow even one of their enemy to die.

The government could not allow women to starve themselves to death and the Pankhursts could not allow anyone to be killed in their bombings and fires.

The second difference between force-feeding and torture is the objective. The objective of the torturer is to punish or extract information from the victim where as the objective of the force feeder is to prevent the patient from killing themselves.

The wardresses may have had little concern for the welfare of the women they were holding down but the fact remains their primary objective was to save their lives because a death in prison would have created a martyr which would have been an enormous propaganda coup for the Suffragettes and would have been used as justification for the backlash that would have certainly followed.

George Dangerfield is often accused of dismissing the pain and damage caused by force-feeding by saying, *"Forcible feeding is no more than extremely unpleasant"* but this is taken out of context. The full quote is, *"If the victim does not resist, forcible feeding is no more than extremely unpleasant, but the Suffragettes were determined to resist."*

THE SUFFRAGETTES - HEROINES OR TERRORISTS?

It took 7 wardresses and 2 doctors to force-feed Lilian Ida Lenton, a struggle that ended with food entering her lungs, which caused her to become seriously ill with Pleurisy. Her case created an outrage among the public and lead to the introduction of the Prisoners Temporary Discharge for Ill Health Act better known as the "Cat and Mouse Act" in April 1913.

The act stated that hunger-striking Suffragettes who had become ill could be released on temporary license to recover their health, and then the security forces would re-arrest them to continue their sentence.

The Cat and Mouse Act solved the problem of Suffragettes dying in prison and becoming martyrs but it also meant they were released from prison and taken to much less secure houses.

Lilian Lenton started by breaking windows then progressed to setting fires in letterboxes, she went on to set fire to the tea rooms at Kew Gardens, a train station, at least one house and her stated intention was to: Burn two buildings a week whenever she was out of prison. The object being to create an absolutely impossible condition of affairs in the country, to prove it was impossible to govern without the consent of the governed.

Lenton was released under the Cat and Mouse Act on numerous occasions only for her to escape from the secure house and set fire to something else.

There is strong condemnation of both force-feeding and the Cat and Mouse Act but faced with hunger striking prisoners like Lenton the authorities were left with very few options. If they gave in to the terrorists (even if they had a just cause) this would set a precedent that would lead to everyone with a cause just or otherwise copying their tactics and indeed many of the tactics used by the Suffragettes are used by terrorists today such as simultaneous multiple attacks, hunger strikes, bombing iconic buildings and using propaganda to draw up the battle lines between themselves and their chosen enemy.

We must remember that at this time there were also calls for home rule in Ireland which ended with extreme terrorism on both sides, so for the Irish, giving in to the terrorists was not even an option.

This chapter starts with the question are the Suffragettes heroines or terrorists?

Terrorism is defined as...

The use or threat of action where the use or threat is designed to influence the government or an international governmental organisation or to intimidate the public or a section of the public and the use or threat is made for the purpose of advancing a political, religious, racial or ideological cause.

Action falls within this subsection if it involves...

THE SUFFRAGETTES - HEROINES OR TERRORISTS?

(a) Serious violence against a person;
(b) Involves serious damage to property;
(c) Endangers a person's life, other than that of the person committing the action;
(d) Creates a serious risk to the health or safety of the public or a section of the public;
(e) Is designed seriously to interfere with or seriously to disrupt an electronic system.

The use or threat of action which involves the use of firearms or explosives is terrorism whether or not subsection (1)(b) of the 2005/06 terrorism act is satisfied.

Any of the above actions will count as an act of terrorism and the Suffragettes were guilty of all of them so their level of violence is more than enough for them to qualify as a terrorist organisation but one man's terrorist is another man's freedom fighter.

Was their situation sufficiently serious to warrant bombing iconic buildings like the British Museum, the Albert Hall, Westminster Abbey, the Royal Observatory or burning down churches, homes, stately homes, railway stations, trains, sports pavilions and all the other violent acts?

I am sure the thousands of working class women who marched behind the Pankhursts believed they were marching for the right for all women to vote which would have been a huge stride forward for democracy and equality in a world in which very few countries had yet given women the vote but the Pankhursts did not want democracy.

The Pankhursts wanted to force the will of the minority onto the majority. The Pankhursts did not want votes for the working class of either gender, they did not want to empower women, they wanted to empower themselves.

The Woman's Socialist Political Union (WSPU) was run as an autocracy, anyone who opposed the cause was attacked, and anyone who questioned the decisions made by the Pankhursts were immediately expelled from the WSPU.

In her 1914 autobiography Emmeline Pankhurst tells how she dismissed criticism of the WSPU's autocratic leadership structure saying...

"If at any time a member, or a group of members, loses faith in our policy; if anyone begins to suggest that some other policy ought to be substituted, or if she tries to confuse the issue by adding other policies, she ceases at once to be a member.

Autocratic? Quite so. But, you may object, a suffrage organisation ought to be democratic.

Well the members of the WSPU do not agree with you. We do not believe in the effectiveness of the ordinary suffrage organisation. The WSPU is not hampered by a complexity of rules. We have no constitution and by-laws, nothing to be amended or tinkered with or quarrelled over at an annual meeting...The WSPU is simply a suffrage army in the field."

THE SUFFRAGETTES - HEROINES OR TERRORISTS?

Christabel Pankhurst said to her sister Sylvia...

"You have your own ideas. We do not want that; We want all our women to take their instructions and walk in step like an army!"

Sylvia was herself later expelled from the WSPU.

Votes for property owning women on a par with property owning men would, I agree have been a small step in the right direction but not enough to warrant this level of violence particularly as there was an established suffrage movement before the emergence of the Suffragettes that had been making progress in persuading many of the men with power that everyone should have the vote.

This progress was too slow for Emmeline and Christabel Pankhurst, which is why they formed the WSPU and with their unquestionable ability they persuaded the women of Britain to rise up and demand the vote. This put women's suffrage at the front of every agenda but this army of women became disenchanted with their leaders.

For many women the autocratic nature of the WSPU was impossible to square with their fight for democracy and they found the accelerating level of violence unacceptable which led to women leaving the WSPU in their thousands.

The Suffragettes did not advance the quest for universal suffrage, they actually set it back.

The Pankhursts insistence on having votes **only** for the wealthy drove a wedge between the WSPU and the Labour party who wanted votes for everyone of working class (including women), enabling them to vote for the new worker's party.

By 1913 the WSPU was reduced to 2,000 members while the older, National Union of Women's Suffrage Societies (one of whose slogans was "*Law-Abiding Suffragists*" as opposed to the Pankhursts' "*Actions Not Words*") led by Millicent Fawcett had 50,000 members.

Millicent Fawcett was a moderate campaigner who distanced herself from the militant and violent activities of the Pankhursts, she believed that their actions were in fact harming women's chances of gaining the vote, as they were alienating many of the MPs who were at that time debating whether or not to give women the vote, as well as souring much of the general public towards the campaign for women's suffrage.

Millicent Fawcett also campaigned to curb child abuse by raising the age of consent, criminalise incest and cruelty to children within the family, to end the practice of excluding women from courtrooms when sexual offences were under consideration, to stamp out the white slave trade, to prevent child marriage and for the introduction of regulated prostitution in India.

Source:
https://en.wikipedia.org/wiki/Millicent_Fawcett

THE SUFFRAGETTES - HEROINES OR TERRORISTS?

It was Millicent Fawcett who used the First World War to bring about changes in attitude.

In the war, the shortage of men meant that women were forced to do 'men's work' while the men were away fighting, proving beyond any doubt that women were quite capable of doing work previously thought to be beyond them.

The war also changed attitudes to wealth and privilege, such things mean nothing in the trenches when rich and poor go over the top side by side.

It is demeaning for a women to be honoured simply for their gender rather than their achievements but if you are looking for a woman worthy of her place in our passports or on our bank notes, you could do a lot worse than the woman who did most to give women the vote, Millicent Fawcett or the woman who gave us refuges for the victims of domestic violence, Erin Pizzey.

When the war ended, the 1918 Representation of the People Act gave woman over the age of 30 the vote, it also removed property restrictions on men's suffrage giving them the vote from the age of 21.

The age difference was because at a time when women greatly out numbered men, parliament could not bring it self to give women the controlling vote after the recent terror campaign waged by the Suffragettes.

It's one thing to give the vote to women but giving the vote to a bunch of terrorists is quite another.

After getting the vote Emmeline and Christabel Pankhurst reinvented the WSPU as the Women's Party, still open only to women.

All this was 100 years ago but with an unelected head of state and an unelected second chamber **women still don't have full suffrage** (men don't either).

Women (and men) are also denied the vote with all woman short lists for political candidates such as 'Blair's Babes' because apart from the obvious employment discrimination we the voters are being told who we can or cannot vote for.

FACT:

Women make up 51% of the population and an even higher proportion of the electorate (males under voting age out number females but because males die younger women of voting age out number men) so in a democracy women hold the balance of power.

If women wanted more women in positions of power all they need do is vote for them, but on the whole women don't vote by gender because they can see the importance of having the right person doing the job not just the right gender.

THE SUFFRAGETTES - HEROINES OR TERRORISTS?

As I write, the most powerful person in the UK is a woman - Theresa May, the most powerful person in Europe is a woman - Angela Merkel and if Hillary Clinton is successful in her second bid for the White House then by the time you read this, three of the most powerful people in the world will be women. (p.s. Clinton won the popular vote with almost 3,000,000 more votes but the electoral college system means that Trump will be the next president).

To me as an equalist, the gender is irrelevant. We need the right people in power and their gender is of no more importance than their shoe size so why all the calls for more women in parliament?

The argument runs...

Women would spend the nations wealth on health and education and would be less likely to send the nation's sons to war while men would spend it on more guns and bigger armies but this is questionable.

As I write the UK has it's second woman as Prime Minister, Theresa May, who's first action as PM was to answer an emphatic *"Yes"* to the question, *"Would she be prepared to push the nuclear button that would kill 100,000 innocent men, women and children."* I have to say here that I would also have answer yes if I were in Theresa May's position. I would never push the button of course but for the deterrent to work it need not be used, or even exist.

Historically we have had only one other woman Prime Minister in the UK, so not a big sample but Margaret Thatcher took the UK into…

The First Gulf War;

The Falklands War;

The Cod War;

Some of the coldest days of the Cold War;

The most troubled days of the Northern Ireland Troubles.

Thatcher also gave us damn near civil war with the miner's strikes and the pole tax riots so the idea that politics would be gentler and less confrontational with more women is at best questionable.

To be fair to Thatcher the country had serious problems and an autocratic leader may even have been the right tool for the job at that time but my point stands, it was her politics that made Thatcher what she was, not her gender.

If you were to ask me to chose between a man or a woman for political office I would have to ask you which man and which woman.

If it were between Hillary Clinton or Donald Trump I would definitely choose the woman but if it were the likes of Sarah Palin or Marine La Pen, they would be very unlikely to get

THE SUFFRAGETTES - HEROINES OR TERRORISTS?

my vote.

There is no doubt that there was discrimination against women a hundred years ago and there still is.

There is no doubt that there was discrimination against men a hundred years ago and there still is.

It is itself discriminatory to tackle discrimination by gender rather than by the effect of the discrimination. When demanding equality for women you don't actually need the 'for women.'

We should all simply be calling for equality. Do the feminists want equality or do they (like the Suffragettes) simply want to redistribute the advantage?

Many feminists call for equality while advocating the opposite with positive discrimination or all women short lists. When questioned about this it seems that what they really want is payback for the centuries of oppression suffered by women but if you went back a hundred years to the time of the Suffragettes would you want to go back as a man or a woman?

As I said in the chapter 'Are men never discriminated against?', a 100 years ago the Suffragettes were fighting for the vote but the men were fighting for their country, half starved in the lousy disease and rat infested trenches of the First World War, rotting from the feet up while being bayoneted, bombed, shot and gassed or if the post traumatic stress all got too much they were taken out and shot for cowardice by their own side and almost half the men in those trenches did not have the vote either.

The premise that it was a man's world is not very accurate. Life was harder then for everyone. The world may be far easier now but we still have discrimination with advantage and disadvantage on both sides.

When being encouraged to "smash the patriarchy" we should remember that women have a voting majority. Women instigate two thirds of divorces yet it's almost always the man who is thrown out of the house by the smaller weaker woman. Women win 90% of custody battles. It's men that disproportionately have their hands on the levers of power in politics and business but in many areas of our lives it looks a lot more like a matriarchy and it's actually the hand that rocks the cradle that is the hand that rules the domestic world.

Chapter 14

Women control the means of reproduction

EQUALITY FOR WOMEN IS AN OXYMORON

Women control the means of reproduction

> "Women lie about being on birth control. Women claim their antibiotics rendered their birth control pills ineffective. Women lie about their menstrual cycles. Women lie and claim they're infertile. They get ex-boyfriends drunk and lure them into bed. They collect sperm from used condoms. They get pregnant by another man and lie about the patternity. This is just wrong. It is wrong! It is wrong! It is wrong! And it's just a glimpse of the hell that is sure to follow."
>
> — Dr Tara J. Palmatier

The above quote should start "**Some** women lie...", as do some men.

Contraception is something the man and the woman must agree on before they have sex.

A man who says he is wearing a condom but is not or sabotages his condom in some way has changed the terms and conditions that the woman agreed to when consenting to sex. In the eyes of the law this constitutes non-consensual sex and therefore rape.

If a man lying about wearing a condom makes consensual sex non-consensual, then surely a woman lying about taking the pill should be looked at in the same way.

If a man tricks a woman into pregnancy, she still has options…

A woman will know long before the baby is due that she is pregnant and can chose to terminate the pregnancy. Many woman may not wish to do this, however termination is very common with 1 in 3 women choosing to have an abortion at some point in their lives.

Source:
http://www.independent.co.uk/life-style/health-and-families/features/1-in-3-women-have-an-abortion-and-95-don't-regret-it-so-why-arent-we-talking-about-it-10392750.html

The woman can also have the baby and then put the baby up for adoption, freeing both the mother and the father from all responsibility for the care and the cost of the child.

A man who has been tricked into conceiving a child on the other hand has no say in what happens next and must comply with whatever the woman decides to do.

A man who deliberately puts a woman in a position where she must decide whether to go through the emotional trauma of a termination or the enormous life changing effects of having a child deserves whatever punishments come his way.

Men may lie about wearing a condom to heighten sensitivity during sex or to trick a woman into motherhood but I believe it is far, far more common for the woman to be the one doing

WOMEN CONTROL THE MEANS OF REPRODUCTION

the tricking.

I once overheard a three-way conversation between a man and two women in which the man complained about being tricked into unwilling fatherhood by his girlfriend. One of the women admitted she had done the same thing, adding she had put her pills down the toilet in case her boyfriend noticed the missed days on her pill card and the second woman said that her friend had also done this.

My conclusion from this very small sample is that a lot of men are fathers through deception.

Before conception both the man and the woman have the same responsibilities and the same right to chose whether sex should lead to parenthood but from the moment of conception this all changes.

If a woman finds out that she has been tricked into pregnancy and unilaterally decides to end the pregnancy she can take Mifepristone and Misoprostol (the abortion pill) for up to 10 weeks after conception without discussing this with the would-be father or even telling him about it.

If a man were to find that he had been tricked into pregnancy and he wanted to unilaterally end the pregnancy by slipping Mifepristone and Misoprostol into the would-be mother's morning tea that would be classed as child destruction, which carries a life sentence.

It's not the despicable act of secretly giving a woman drugs that carries the life sentence it's the killing of an unborn child without the mother's consent.

The effects of abortion or childbirth on a woman's body make it far more serious for the woman and for that reason it is right that the woman gets the final say as to whether or not the pregnancy continues but is it right that the father gets no say at all?

Is it right that a man who is deliberately duped into fatherhood should have to accept the consequences of becoming a father while the mother is free to unilaterally decide to have a child by deception and then force the man to pay for it?

In one such case a woman who wanted a baby admitted she had taken a discarded condom and used it's contents to get pregnant. Apart from the emotional cost, the father estimates he will have to pay £80,000 for her actions because regardless of how it got there, the rule is, if there is DNA the man must pay.

Source:
http://www.dailymail.co.uk/femail/article-2059548/Four-men-reveal-trauma-dad-deception.html

This is fraud, aided and abetted by the child maintenance enforcement agencies where the money is forcibly collected by the state and given to the fraudster and as the amount you pay depends on how much you earn not the cost of bringing up the child, getting pregnant by a rich man could be quite lucrative, although I think most women do it for the baby not the money.

There are some women who are not pregnant but would like someone to think that they are.

In recent years with the help of the Internet the 'sham pregnancy' seems to have become big business. You can now easily buy a positive pregnancy test online. It seems some pregnant women are selling positive tests to women who are not pregnant but want to convince someone that they are.

The fake positive pregnancy test business has moved on to the point that you can now get a test that has been specifically made for this purpose and will change to show a positive result in front of your eyes if made wet with anything even tap water. You can also now get fake scan photos in 2D or the new 3D format with your name and your doctor's name printed on them.

Source:
https://www.amazon.com/Prank-Pregnancy-Always-Turns-Positive/dp/B00YQDGFLK

When they first appeared, the positive tests were sold as a way to encourage your boyfriend to, 'pop the question' but this raised legal and moral questions so now they are normally advertised as a prank, however what they are actually used for has probably not changed much.

A proposal of marriage based on deception is not a very good way to start a lifetime together but worse than that are the women who use the positive tests as a way to extort money.

Some women have asked for the cost of an abortion or medical costs while some have gone even further…

I recently read the case of a woman who told her ex that she had had the baby and she even went as far as to borrow a friend's baby in order to claim maintenance payments for her non-existent child.

I am not trying to suggest that all women are deceitful, most are not but where they are found to be defrauding men out of very large sums of money, I ask that this crime be taken seriously rather than just ignored completely or treated as just bad luck on the part of the man, as it is in the misattributing of the 'Cuckoo kids.'

Chapter 15

Cuckoo kids

EQUALITY FOR WOMEN IS AN OXYMORON

Cuckoo kids

"It is a wise father that knows his own child."
WILLIAM SHAKESPEARE

I have never heard of any women ever being arrested for putting the wrong father's name on a birth certificate.

If a woman lies about the paternity of her child the taxpayer pays for the DNA test. If she is telling the truth the father must pay about £250.00 for a DNA test, either way the mother pays nothing so with no cost to the mother and no risk of prosecution, why not lie?

It is easy to find data for the number of negative paternity tests but it is impossible to accurately estimate the true number of misattributed children in the UK.

Estimates for the number of men who are not biologically related to 'their' children range from between 2% right up to over 30% with the number of negative results for DNA tests requested by fathers (or not) through the CSA coming out at somewhere between 16% and 19%.

Source:
http://www.dailymail.co.uk/news/article-2085950/Women-forced-pay-paternity-tests-prove-identity-fathers-CSA-battles.html

In the 10 years between 1998 and 2008 DNA tests exposed

almost 5,000 false paternity claims but this is just the tip of the iceberg since most children are not the subject of a paternity claim and of those who are, most are never DNA tested.

Source:
http://www.dailymail.co.uk/news/article-1040589/One-CSA-mothers-wrong-father.html

The numbers for the misattributed children are distorted on one side because men who ask for a paternity test will probably already have their suspicions and the numbers are also distorted on the other side by the women who name the wrong man as the father on the birth certificate wanting to keep their secret.

Women who misattribute their children are also committing an offence, so are much less likely to take part in any study that may expose their deceit and their crime even though women are never prosecuted for this offence.

The only way to get the true figure would be to routinely DNA test all babies at birth.

If we take the lowest end of the estimates, that would still mean that there are around a million misattributed people in the UK.

I say people and not children because some of the consequences of this crime continue throughout life and on into the following generations.

CUCKOO KIDS

If a woman has an affair and gets pregnant by her lover the best solution is probably to quietly have a termination but if she decides to keep the baby, she will almost certainly tell her husband the baby is his.

This is doubly unfair on her husband who has not only been cheated on but then conned into bringing up her lover's child but for the child this may sometimes be the best outcome.

A child with two parents will normally do better than a child brought up in a one-parent family even if the child is not biologically related to the 'father' but it is only ever in the best interest of the child from the point where the mother is already pregnant.

If I were advising a friend who had found herself 'accidentally' pregnant by a man other than her husband and she wouldn't or couldn't have a termination, I think I would probably tell her to misattribute the baby, after all if her husband remains blissfully unaware then where is the harm?

There is harm of course and not just to the duped husband, but also the child and the biological father.

For every cuckoo kid there are at least three victims.

The child is harmed because:

The truth about who is the child's father may never come out but if it does it is often when the 'parents' separate, so the child has both the trauma of their parents break up and the trauma of finding out that one of the two people they trusted and relied on for everything has lied to them and the other person is not actually their father and he may well disappear from their lives.

The truth about who is related to whom may also come out when a man dies.

If a man leaves the family firm to his eldest son or daughter whom he has worked with, building up the business side by side for 40 years, then he knows his life's work will be left in safe hands but if it turns out that his son is not his son, then his estate will not be divided as he intended and the business will probably have to be sold to pay the lawyers to sort out the mess.

It is not just the confusion over inheritance that the misattributed person will now have to deal with. At a time of bereavement he now finds he has never met his biological father who may now be dead and his feelings for his mother may also change when he finds out she has lied to his non-biological father and to him for all his life.

The misattributed person will also have given false information to his doctor...

Your risk of dying from many diseases including cancers vary greatly depending on your family history which in turn depends on who is actually in your family.

If my doctor were to ask me if there is any history of testicular cancer in the family my answer will be "*No, none at all*" but the milkman died of it, as did his father, grandfather, 2 uncles and 3 brothers so should it turn out that my biological father is actually the milkman then my families medical history will look very different.

Not knowing who is in your family may have other consequences...

The Madness song, Shame and Scandal, tells the tail of a young man who finds a girl he likes but his father tells him...

"No! The girl is your sister, but your mama don't know."

His mother then laughs and says...

"Go man go, your daddy ain't your daddy, but your daddy don't know."

With so many "Cuckoo Kids" not knowing who their real parents are, how many of us are in a relationship with someone who is too closely related to us to be healthy or even legal?

The non-biological father is harmed because:

For many people having your own child is of supreme importance.

The NHS spends 400 million a year on IVF with many more couple paying up to £6,000 privately for each cycle.

When a child is misattributed then a man that thought himself a family man may find out too late that he is in fact childless.

Source:
http://www.bbc.com/news/health-34658354

When a 'father' is given the wrong child to bring up it's a non-event.

Despite the obvious emotional distress and financial loss suffered by a man who finds out that a child is not his, if the truth should ever come to light, there will be no compensation, no inquiry and it won't even make one line in the local paper. In contrast, in the rare cases where the tables are turned and it's the mother that has been given the wrong baby in a hospital mix-up, then it is all taken very seriously with mass media coverage and million pound law suits.

Source:
http://www.dailymail.co.uk/news/article-2947522/Two-couples-discovered-given-wrong-babies-TEN-YEARS-daughters-born-awarded-2million-euros-French-court.html

Some life changing decisions may depend on whether or not a man already has a child. IVF or vasectomy and inheritance will depend on how many children he believes he has.

The biological father is harmed because:

The biological father looses the chance to know his child or even know of their existence.

Again, life-changing decisions depend on whether or not a man has a child.

A man may choose vasectomy instead of IVF or he may wish to favour his children over the cats home in his will and with the rise of living organ donation, as a blood relative he may even wish to give his child or grandchild a kidney or a part of his liver.

Others are harmed because:

Grandparents may never know of a longed for grandchild.

Blood relatives will not be forewarned about medical risks in the family and false blood relatives will be giving their doctors false information.

What at first glance may look like a victimless crime is in truth a crime where everyone looses and no one wins.

The mother gains nothing she has not secured a provider for her child but simply swapped one for another, the biological father never gets to bring up his child, the husband is duped into bringing up another man's child and as we have seen there are many risks to the child so if no-one wins, why is it so common?

The best husband and the best father for your children are biologically not the same.

To secure the best life chances for her children and grandchildren a woman needs to marry a good dependable provider but to produce the most grandchildren she needs an unreliable high testosterone male to father her children because his unreliable high testosterone male children will be much more likely to have affairs and produce lots of "Cuckoo Kids" all over town.

There has been some interesting research including that of Professor David Perret of St Andrew's University that suggests this is indeed what happens and that women are biologically programmed to choose different men for the two different roles.

In a 1999 BBC World News item, Professor Perret said that, *"Women are attracted to more masculine-looking men at the most fertile time of their menstrual cycle but during the less fertile times, they choose men with more feminine-looking faces."* The controversial implication of this research is that, in evolutionary terms, it is natural for a woman to be unfaithful in order to secure both the best genes and the best provider for her children.

Source:
http://news.bbc.co.uk/2/hi/376321.stm

So a woman is programmed to have affairs, well here's a news flash, so are men, they are programmed to make babies with every woman that will let them.

This all makes perfect biological sense and may help to explain the high numbers of misattributed children but in today's over-populated world it's quality not quantity that is important and having as many children as possible is no longer what is needed and what of justice?

Nature tells us to eat too much salt, eat too much sugar, eat too much fat and make as many babies as we can, This is not good for us as individuals or for society.

In today's world we can easily control who we have children with. We don't need to give in to these influences. We can chose the rules we live by and although in some cases the injustice of a misattributed child may be trumped by the welfare of the child, with a non-biological father being better than none, the best situation for the child will almost always be, to be with both his biological parents who are in a stable relationship, so for that reason I would welcome DNA tests at birth to confirm the true parentage of all children.

DNA tests at birth will...

    End the injustices of misattributed babies;

    End the trauma of finding out your father is not your

father;

End the trauma of finding out your child is not your child;

Enable doctors to accurately assess health risks;

Avoid the risk of inadvertently marrying your half sibling;

Allow us all to know who we are;

Allow the state to correctly assess who should be paying for whom without the need for a man to effectively say, "*I don't think you are mine and I won't pay for you until you prove it*", to the children he loves and has cared for all their lives and who themselves have just suffered the trauma of their parents break up. A man would need to have real doubts before putting himself and 'his' children through that.

Chapter 16

Why should I pay for your dog?

EQUALITY FOR WOMEN IS AN OXYMORON

Why should I pay for your dog?

"Large families were a poor man's form of social security."

Richard Tames

If my lifestyle choice were to have a dog I would not then ask you or anyone else to help pay for it. I would check I could afford a dog before going to the pet shop and if I couldn't afford to keep it I would simply have to wait until my resources were sufficient to meet my aspiration of becoming a dog owner!

So if I wouldn't expect you to pay for my dog, why should I, as a taxpayer, pay for your kids?

The analogy of a dog vs a child is often put forward as in the statement *"You wouldn't pay for my dog so why should I pay for your children"* but in purely economic terms a dog and a child are quite different.

When a man who was previously childless and had only himself to keep, decides to have a child, his whole life changes out of all recognition. A child takes up most of his time and all of his money. He doesn't just have an extra mouth to feed, he needs a mountain of equipment, prams, cots, clothes, a bigger house, a car instead of a bike, the list goes on.

He also needs to make up for his partner's lost earnings. The baby will make a massive call on his time too, leaving him less time to earn. All new parents are late for everything, until they get used to how long it takes to get out of the house with a baby.

Babies need to be fed, cleaned and changed before you go out. They need to be transferred to the car seat. The pram needs to be folded and stored, then got out and unfolded on arrival and the baby transferred back into it. You need to pack as if you were going on holiday for even the shortest of trips out. You need food, warm clothing in case it gets cold, spare clothing in case of accidents, dummy, change bag… *"Ready!"*

"Oh, it's lunch time, do you want to eat before we go?"

For parents on anything less than a good wage the loss of one wage and the extra cost of a baby will mean a lot of belt tightening, that's why the state helps almost all parents with handouts and benefits of one sort or another but is it right that taxpayers without children should be subsidising the lifestyle choices of those who decide to have them?

If you were to ask me, would I pay for your dog?

The answer might actually be yes but only in very special circumstances, for instance…

If you bought a dog as a pet or for protection then sorry you are on your own, but consider this scenario.

You buy yourself a dog. The dog sniffs and worries at a patch of discoloured skin on your leg. You mention this to your doctor, who has read about dogs being able to smell cancer. He sends you for tests that come back positive. The cancer was detected very early so after a minor operation you get the all clear.

You train your dog to do this on other people. The word goes round and people come to your dog for a life saving medical opinion.

Many people have their lives saved through early diagnosis and most of them would like to show their gratitude with a gift but dogs can't spend money, so the grateful patients arrange with the butcher to provide a lifetime's supply of bones or with the kennel maid for an hour a day of fetch, long walks and the like.

The patients give you nothing! After all it's the dog that is doing the work isn't it?

How do you feel about this?

Shouldn't you get some of the profit? When all's said and done it's your dog and you have put a lot into it:

> You bought the puppy;
> You bought his food and paid for his jabs;

EQUALITY FOR WOMEN IS AN OXYMORON

>You bought a lead, bowls, a basket and a kennel;
>You house trained him and cleaned up the mess;
>You walked him, trained him and cared for him;
>You paid for obedience classes, etc.

After all this are you really entitled to nothing in return?

We are happy to pay for dogs when they are working for us. We would all be quite happy to pay for this dog in our taxes just as we do for the sniffer dogs looking for bombs or drugs and don't forget all the guide dogs or the Saint Bernard with his keg of brandy.

Now substitute the dog for a child…

All the things you bought, represents the enormous cost of a child.

For "house training and cleaning up the mess" read potty training.

Substitute the obedience training, for all the things parent's teach their children which is not just help with homework or paying for university but also teaching him to walk, talk and eat with a knife and fork.

The caring is all the hours of work put in to bring up a child plus the rest of your time on call.

After all this, are the parents really entitled to nothing?

Consider this scenario…

Two retired people go to a shop to buy a loaf of bread. One is a parent the other is not. They each give the baker a pound and receive their loaf.

To produce bread you need flour, water, yeast, salt and a baker. They have both paid for the ingredients and a portion of the baker's wages but by bringing up a child the parent has also done her bit to produce the generation of workers that include the baker.

Without bakers there would be no bread, well perhaps most people could knock up a loaf of bread if they had to but not so easy to replace your own hip should the need arise.

Consider the farmer…

The fact is, work doesn't just stop when we stop working. A farmer cannot just hang up the keys to his tractor and retire, he must pass them on to his son or his daughter because without farmers none of us will eat!

Children are not just a lifestyle choice. We need the next generation!

We must all invest work today to produce the workers of tomorrow.

Still not convinced?

Consider a time before money confused the issue, or consider a lost tribe in the Amazon Rainforest yet to invent it.

If you were a child born to this tribe you would be provided for and cared for by your parents. You would be a burden on them.

When you grow up and have children of your own the burden is then yours to carry.

When your children grow up, you care for your elderly parents who are now unproductive and a burden.

When your parents die, you are once more the burden and must rely on your children to provide for you, in your old age.

In this way you are a burden in childhood and in old age, but you have carried that burden for your children and for your parents - **You leave this world break-even.**

If you lived in this tribe but did not have children, you will not be able to cash in the investment that the parents made when bringing up their children. When you are too old to provide for yourself, you will have to rely on the charity of the tribe or starve to death.

You will have been a burden twice but carried the burden only once - **You will leave this world in debt or early.**

If you make the lifestyle choice to opt out of the enormous cost and work involved in bringing up the next generation do you still have the right to benefit from the fruits of their labour?

The question *"Why should I pay for your dog?"* Becomes *"Why should you have the benefit of my dog?"*

The confusion stems from the way in which people regard children. We often think of children as possessions comparable to the dog.

A dog of course is a possession. We can buy it, sell it, even have it put down if we so choose but is a child ever a possession or are they an individual in his or her own right?

For me a child is NEVER a possession but for the *"Why should I pay for your child?"* people and also the state, their status changes.

While a child is an expense and a burden they are 'your child', "You had it now you look after it, you wanted it, you pay for it."

As soon as the child reaches working age and becomes an asset we are now quite happy to consider them as an individual who must work and pay their taxes to the state rather than to their former owners (their parents).

If when at the age of 17, 18, or 19 a child gets into trouble we may still think it's the responsibility of the parents to punish him or compensate us for a broken window or a spray painted wall.

Most bizarre of all is that we expect a 17 or 18 year old who is earning, to share his earnings with the state via his taxes, with any money that goes to his parents, being for food and lodgings but if he should then loose his job and once again becomes a financial burden, he instantly reverts back to being the responsibility of his parents and it is they who must provide for him, that is until he finds work and once more becomes an asset, then like magic he turns back into a productive member of society and again we want our share of his wages.

It is inevitable that we will soon have to stop asking who pays for whom and instead we will all (as far as is possible) be expected to pay our own way.

It is inevitable that we are going to have to stop asking fathers to financially support themselves, their children and their wives during the childcare years.

It is inevitable that we are going to have to stop asking women to do most of the caring for both the young and the old, preventing them from becoming financially self-sufficient.

We need to spread the cost of bringing up the next generation more fairly and devise a financial system where everyone pays the cost of one childhood and one retirement.

EQUALITY FOR WOMEN IS AN OXYMORON

Chapter 17

Women should not expect equal pay!

EQUALITY FOR WOMEN IS AN OXYMORON

Women should not expect equal pay!

"A successful man is one who makes more money than his wife can spend.

A successful woman is one who can find such a man."

Lana Turner

Women should not expect equal pay and what's more they probably wouldn't want it!

This may seem like an outrageous thing to say but please, don't throw the book against the wall until you have at least heard the arguments.

Question:

Why would women not want equal pay?

Answer:

Because equal pay is only one side of the equation. If you have equal pay you must also have...

> Equality in paying into both the home and the state;
>
> Equality in the amounts of paid work you do;
>
> Equality in the types of work you do.

FACT:

Men earn more because they need to.

The fact is men may earn more, yet women spend more, this is because there is a flood of money going…

> From men to women;
>
> From men to children;
>
> From men to the taxman.

The paying gap is a fact that is seldom mentioned in the debates over equal pay but from *"Can I buy you a drink?"* on the very first date, to the final divorce settlement, it's men doing the paying.

On many dating sites women can join for free and some nightclubs still offer women free entry and/or free drinks (this is illegal but never enforced).

Source:
http://www.girlsdateforfree.com/
https://www.forbes.com/sites/bridgetbrennan/2015/01/21/top-10-things-everyone-should-know-about-women-consumers/#1172e6e06a8b

Who gets to earn the most money, is far less important than who gets the benefit of the money. For men and to a lesser extent women, their earnings are immediately redistributed.

In most families it's the man who is the main breadwinner,

WOMEN SHOULD NOT EXPECT EQUAL PAY!

which means his earnings are shared between the whole family.

When a baby arrives, fathers need to work more to provide for both mother and child while the mothers no longer have the time to put in the hours they worked before the arrival of the baby.

The need to provide for their family is the reason fathers earn more than childless men.

When my first child was on the way, the first person I told was my boss. I told him I was going to need more overtime, a promotion or both.

The Metro described this extra money as a *"wage bonus."* A bonus is not the way I would describe having to work longer and harder to meet other people's needs.

Source:
http://metro.co.uk/2016/04/25/men-with-children-earn-more-than-those-without-5838317/

Consider the Average family...

Mr and Mrs Average work at the same place doing the same job. They each do forty hours a week and receive the same pay. They do this for five years.

So far, so good.

After five years Mrs Average stops work to have children. Mr Average concerned about the drop in the family income with an extra mouth to feed, asks for overtime and is given an extra twenty hours a week, paid at time and a half.

After ten years Mr Average has worked two and a half times as many hours as his wife and has earned two and three quarter times as much money.

On paper the man has earned more money than the woman and earned it at a faster rate for the same job.

Ask yourself this, has Mrs Average been short-changed here?

Bear in mind, all the earnings for both Mr and Mrs Average have gone into a joint account. Despite her lower earnings Mrs Average has had exactly the same access to all the family income.

The house keeping comes out of the joint account, the joint mortgage is paid out of the joint account and if the family goes on holiday, Mrs Average goes too. In short for the last five years Mr Average has put the money into the account while they both take it out equally and if their marriage were to fail, the house and all other assets would be deemed to be jointly owned and Mr Average would be asked or if necessary, forced to continue to pay for his wife and child.

Of course it has to be said here that when I stated Mrs

WOMEN SHOULD NOT EXPECT EQUAL PAY!

Average stopped work to have children nothing could be further from the truth. Children are very hard work and Mrs Average may well have worked as hard or harder than her husband, what she actually did was give up PAID work.

By doing the lions share of the unpaid work Mrs Average made it possible for her husband to do his sixty hour week and she has earned her share of the family income but of course this doesn't show up on paper.

These anomalies can all be straightened out by equally sharing the paid work and the unpaid work (in this case the childcare).

The Averages would then be earning the same, each doing a thirty hour week and sharing the childcare equally.

Is a 30 hour week feasible? Well yes they do a 35 hour week in France but it is becoming more and more difficult to maintain while they have to compete commercially with countries like the UK who allow their workers to work very long hours by opting out of the EU Working Time Directive. This is sold to the workers as a victory over the meddling Europeans, certainly it makes the UK more competitive, but it condemns the work force to a life of juggling work and children to the benefit of neither. There is no point in being richer if your life is poorer.

The flow of money is not only going from men to women who are in a relationship but it is also disproportionately taken from men and given to women by the state in the form of tax.

Men of working age are far more likely than women to be working full time.

Male full time workers, work longer hours and at the moment men still work more years, they also get higher pay. All this means they pay far more in tax.

According to 'Full Fact' the tax bill for men is £92 billion while women only pay £36.8 billion that's a difference of over £55 billion a year.

Men also pay more in national insurance. When a man has paid his full national insurance contributions, he keeps on paying for no extra benefit whereas a great many women don't work enough years to pay their full national insurance contributions.

Source:
http://www.ons.gov.uk/employmentandlabourmarket/peopleinwork/employmentandemployeetypes/bulletins/uklabourmarket/february2016
https://fullfact.org/economy/are-women-paying-60-less-income-tax-men/

The extra tax money is then disproportionately paid back to women because women are more likely to be on benefits and they spend much more time in retirement both because they retire younger and also because they then go on to live over 4 years longer than men.

WOMEN SHOULD NOT EXPECT EQUAL PAY!

The fact is, during the years of childcare almost all women receive all or part of their income from either a man or the state, this fact means that men must earn more and women can afford to earn less and this is one of the main drivers of the wage gap.

This is in no way a criticism of women but pay and paying are two sides of the same equation and inextricably linked. If we want pay parity then this fact must always be recognised and tackled when working to close the pay gap.

A man cannot afford to take a low paid job while he has a wife and family to support but for the supported women the position is reversed.

Women with children who have all or part of their financial needs met by a partner or by the state do not need to earn a 'living wage' in order for them to benefit from work. Consequently there is an army of women, willing and able to do low paid, unskilled, part time work because for them it makes good economic sense and it is the availability of these workers that holds their pay rate down but is it fair, that 'women's work' should be paid at a lower rate than 'men's work'?

In many cases the answer to this question is yes, it is fair that women's work is lower paid because they do different work and have different work patterns but this is dependent on the work not the gender of the worker.

Question:

Should a man and a woman doing the same work get the same pay?

Answer:

Yes of course, what a silly question!

When we are told, women are paid almost 10% less than men, most people assume this is for the same or equivalent work but this is not so!

The pay gap refers not to rates of pay for the same work or annual take-home-pay, it refers to the average hourly rate of pay by gender for all work and the need for men to earn more money means that even where men and women are doing the same job, their work pattern is often quite different and this has a profound affect on pay rates.

FACT:

Men are far more likely to work at night.

Of course there are women who work at night - Police Officers, Nurses, etc., but they make up a small proportion of the workforce with most night work being done by men and therefore most of the night rate premium goes to men.

If more women work nights their average earnings will go

WOMEN SHOULD NOT EXPECT EQUAL PAY!

up, but do women want to work more nights or unsociable hours? If so they deserve the premium that goes with it, the same premium the men get, after all night work messes up your body clock leaving you feeling permanently jet-lagged.

FACT:

Men work longer hours than women.

Men doing full time work, do on average eight hours a week more than women who are doing full time work. That's the equivalent of one extra day a week, or about ten weeks holiday a year, assuming an eight hour day and a five day week.

If you work overtime, there is normally a premium for this, say time and a half.

Men work longer hours with more overtime, therefore they end up being paid more and they also get a higher rate of pay. Women could reduce the earnings gap by doing more overtime.

FACT:

Women do less of the dangerous work so men are much more likely to die at work or because of it!

Source:
https://www.theguardian.com/news/datablog/2013/may/07/men-gender-

divide-feminism

'Equal Pay Day' is held every year to mark the point in the year that women would stop earning if they were paid at the same hourly rate as men. For 2015 this day was set at the 9th of November.

Source:
http://www.fawcettsociety.org.uk/our-work/campaigns/equal-pay-day-2/

'Equal Fatal Injuries at Work Day' was introduced into the UK by the journalist Ally Fogg to mark the point in the year that men would stop dying if they died at the same rate as women. The date for this was set at the 10th of January, less than one third of the way through the first month.

If you do a job that is dangerous, you would expect 'danger money' wouldn't you?

Men do a higher proportion of dangerous work (many of them being injured or dying in the process) therefore they get a higher proportion of the danger money which again distorts average earnings in favour of men.

Women demand pay parity but be careful what you wish for! Danger money, shift premium and overtime rate all mean higher pay rates for men but at a price.

Working Long hours shortens your life.

WOMEN SHOULD NOT EXPECT EQUAL PAY!

Shift work reduces your life expectancy by about 5 years.

Dangerous work does what it says on the tin and men do not only die more often than women while at work, many men also die younger because of it.

Would the feminists be happier with higher wages, if a higher number of women dying at work was the price they had to pay?

If the answer is yes then women are quite welcome to apply to be Fisherwomen, Bomb Disposal Persons, Oil or Gas Riggers, Deep-sea Divers, Dustwomen or Construction Workers. This would not only help to equalise wages but also equalise the fatalities at work rate too!

Women choose the work they do.

Women do the low paid jobs because they can and because it fits in with their family life.

Under the rules of the free market the rate of pay for any job is the least the employer needs to pay and still find enough people of the right quality to fill the vacancies.

Many women prioritise their family over their career and the availability of millions of mothers able to work for low pay, drives down the average pay for 'women's work'.

Two jobs that were judged to be of equal value yet paid at different rates were dust-MEN and dinner-LADIES.

FACT:

Dustman is the 3rd most dangerous job in the UK.

Source:
http://www.mirror.co.uk/lifestyle/top-5-most-dangerous-jobs-5014470

Equalising the pay of dustmen and dinnerladies meant that councils were forced to pay crippling amounts of back pay to all the women who it was said had suffered sex discrimination. Sex discrimination requires that someone is discriminating by gender but in this case it was the women themselves that were choosing the lower paid work.

If a woman wanted to take a job as a dust-lady, I don't believe that a council personnel department (most of whom are women in my experience) would discriminate by gender.

If a man wanted to be a dinner-man he would probably be asked a lot of awkward questions as to why a man wanted to work with children but in theory at least, both jobs are equally available to both genders.

By choosing to become dinner-ladies, women are self-selecting the lower pay so where is the discrimination?

In an equal society a woman who wanted to earn more

WOMEN SHOULD NOT EXPECT EQUAL PAY!

money should not have applied for the lower paid job but our society is not equal. The paid and the unpaid work is not distributed equally.

Women do twice as much of the unpaid work caring for children or the elderly so cannot meet the requirements of a higher-paid full time job, plus overtime and travel.

Men on the other hand are normally the main breadwinner so cannot afford to take a low paid part time job.

Put simply, in most cases...

When a man looks at a job he asks himself if he and his family can live on the money?

When a woman looks at a job she asks herself, can I fit it in round the childcare?

A mother seeking work will see a job as a dinner lady for twenty hours a week (all in school time) as perfect, but a man would need to take on another part time job in order to make up the money.

A father seeking work will see a job as a dustman as perfect as with overtime it will bring in enough money to meet his family's needs, but a woman working as a dust-lady would have to pay most of her wages to a child-minder making the whole thing pointless.

The enemy of equal pay is not a mythical army of misogynistic employers hell-bent on keeping women in their place by paying them less. The enemy is the paid work and the unpaid work gender gap.

If we take out of the equation the need for women to adjust their work pattern to fit in with childcare, then **women are actually doing better than men**.

FACT:

11% of men and 41% of women work part time.

FACT:

Men in part time work get 6.5% LESS per hour than women in part time work.

FACT:

Between the ages of 22-29 women earn MORE than men.

FACT:

Women who do not take a career break earn MORE than men.

Source:
http://visual.ons.gov.uk/what-is-the-gender-pay-gap/

WOMEN SHOULD NOT EXPECT EQUAL PAY!

A man working full-time will earn more than a woman working part time but when they are both working part time it's women that earn more.

If a man and woman left education 15 years ago with the same qualifications, the man will become more valuable to an employer because he has 15 years experience in the field where as the woman has only 5 years experience which is 10 years out of date because she stopped working to bring up her children, she will now be less valuable to an employer than the man, but women who do not take a career break earn more than men.

It is women not men that give up work to bring up the children because the wage gap means that women's low wages make it a financial necessity for the high earning man not the low earning woman to be the main breadwinner... NOT SO!

At the age most women are having their first child (22-29) women are earning more than men.

Women are now leaving education with more qualifications than men and getting the higher pay that goes with it. This is surely good news for women but is it? The reality is men don't usually get to spend the extra money they earn and if women become the main breadwinners they won't get to spend their extra earnings either.

The fact is, as things stand, it's a woman's prerogative to

chose whether or not she continues working after having a child.

It is now acceptable for a woman to continue working and pass the childcare to an au pair, a nanny, a nursery, a childminder, a relative or even the father.

If a woman is well paid she can pay part of her wages to a nursery and continue working. If a woman is low paid she can pay all her wages to a nursery and continue working.

Going to work then giving all your money to someone else to look after your child may not sound like much of a choice but it is pretty close to the deal that men get. The only difference is that for men the carer is normally the child's mother.

If the trend of women earning higher pay than men continues then one of two things will happen. Either women will loose their accepted right to give up work and become a full-time mother with the new expectation being that the higher wage earner will automatically take on the role of provider with the lower wage earner taking on the role of carer or more likely, women will continue to put their careers on hold while they bring up their children regardless of who is the higher earner.

In the second scenario men will be disadvantaged because they will be less well qualified and less well paid.

WOMEN SHOULD NOT EXPECT EQUAL PAY!

The country will be disadvantaged because many of it's highly qualified women will still be doing part time top-up jobs as dinnerladies and cleaners with the less qualified men still making up the bulk of the country's now less qualified and less competitive workforce.

Women will be disadvantaged because the lower paid men will be less able to support them and their children. The men will also pay in less tax so the state will have less money to support them with benefits.

The only way to end the pay gap between the breadwinner and the top-up earner is to share the paid and unpaid work fairly but the pay gap has another cause. There is an enormous gap between the under paid and the over paid.

FACT:

At the bottom of the pay scale there is **no** pay gap.

The biggest pay gap is not the almost 10% gap between men and women, it's the gap between the low paid and the top earners.

At the bottom of the pay scale men and women are paid the same, they both get minimum wage but almost all the highest paying jobs are done by men and this has a huge affect on the average hourly pay rate for men and women.

If a woman on average earnings for a woman, earns 10%

less than her twin brother who is on average earnings for a man then after 10 years he will have earned an entire year's wages more than his sister.

If a woman works 40 hours a week on minimum wage at the bottom end of the earnings spectrum and her brother is one of the top earners as a CEO of one of the FTSE top 100 companies then after 10 years he will have earned the equivalent of 3,312 years wages more than his sister.

I have based these figures on the 2016 minimum wage of almost £15,00 a year for someone over 25 years old and top FTSE pay of just under £5 million a year.

Source:
http://www.express.co.uk/finance/city/631605/UK-FTSE-bosses-paid-more-two-days-average-worker-earns-year

We cannot expect a cleaner to be paid the same as the chief executive and we cannot expect many women to become the chief executive if they don't put in the same hours as the other people that are trying to make it to the top of the corporate ladder.

Low paid work will be with us as long as there are people available and willing to do it and it will be women that are doing most of the low paid work as long as, in the words of Genesis *"Dad does the office and Mum does the washing."* whatever the rules on equal pay and advertising jobs for both sexes may be.
I hear and agree with all the calls for more women in the

boardroom but most working men are not in the boardroom either.

Wage equality also means:

> More women risking their lives up scaffolds and down mines;
>
> Equality in pay and paying;
>
> Balancing the paid and unpaid work;
>
> Balancing of the unsociable hours worked;
>
> Reducing the gap between the top wage earners and those at the bottom.

EQUALITY FOR WOMEN IS AN OXYMORON

Chapter 18

The self-inflicted glass ceiling

EQUALITY FOR WOMEN IS AN OXYMORON

The self-inflicted glass ceiling

"I could be working for another 25 years and am only likely to be reading bedtime stories for another two or three years.".

YVETTE COOPER

When asked if she would be running in the Labour leadership contest

Source:
https://www.theguardian.com/commentisfree/2010/may/28/yvette-cooper-labour-leadership
http://www.bbc.com/news/uk-politics-33692930

Many women, when given the choice of family or career, choose family. This is a choice rarely afforded to most men unless they have a partner who is willing and can afford to take on the normally male role of breadwinner.

Yvette Cooper is an example of the self-inflicted glass ceiling. In the 2010 leadership contest for the Labour party she was asked whether she would be standing, giving her party the opportunity to vote for a woman candidate.

Her answer was telling, she said she would not stand because she had children of bedtime story age and thought the extra work of party leader would not leave her enough time for her children. She said this despite the previous three Prime Ministers (all men) each having bedtime story age children so Yvette, it is in some part your fault women are under represented in the top jobs however I am in no way criticising your choice I am simply pointing out that it was **your** choice and not a glass ceiling that prevented you becoming party leader and maybe Prime Minister.

I am quite convinced that women would welcome the chance to become financially independent and men would welcome the chance to have equal involvement in family life but if we want women to take their rightful place at the top in politics or any other job, then they need to prioritise their careers over their families to the same level that men do but once again it's our system of woman-carer and man-provider role division that makes this so difficult.

If women put their careers on hold for years to have children, they can't then expect to return to the work place at the level they would have been at if they hadn't broken their service, or can they?

A woman who has been out of the work place for many years will have become 'rusty' and will never be as 'right for the job' as a man or a woman for that matter, who has kept up-to-date and gained more experience but recently there have been calls to give women the right not just to have their job held open for them but to be taken back at the level they would have been at if they had not taken a career break.

Women who work their way up the corporate ladder gaining the relevant skills and experience on the way are quite capable of doing the top jobs but the only way to get both the right person and more women at the top is to have more 'time served' women to choose from and to do this we need to break the gender bias in the provider/carer roles.

If we have all woman shortlists and employers are forced to allocate the top jobs by gender instead of relevant experience and proven capability, this will be damaging for employers, the other employees and the national economy.

If employers are forced to take women back at the level they would have reached after a career break then they will have to put inexperienced people in the positions that require experience.

If we take this to it's logical conclusion employers who are forced to give preferential treatment to returning women will be reluctant to take on women in the first place so they will also need to be forced to take on equal numbers of men and women and it will all end with some very capable women being given extra training and the opportunity to reach their full potential while others would be put into positions they would never have reached by there own merits and would have to be 'babysat' by someone with the relevant experience.

A secondary effect of this is that many of these returning mothers will be taking the jobs that would previously have gone to the next generation of breadwinners, the very men that the next generation of mothers will rely on to provide for them and their children while they are doing the caring.

The Yvette Cooper case is high profile but the self-inflicted glass ceiling is evident at all levels and not only for women to spend more time with their children.

For many women there is no financial imperative to work at all. If their husband's earn good money, many women chose not to work or continue to only work part time long after the children have grown up.

Example:

I once worked as a department manager in a supermarket. Part of my job was to give the staff an annual appraisal. At the end of the appraisal I would ask the obligatory question, *"Where do you see yourself one year from now?"*

The men would joke saying something like, *"Doing your job!"*. They were mostly full timers, there to earn a living with an eye to promotion and more money.

The women would say, *"Sitting here doing another pointless appraisal with you"*. They were there doing a low stress part time job to earn a bit of extra money. They had no inclination to progress in the company or change things in any way.

When offered the possibility of more hours or responsibility they would say, *"No thanks, it suits me as I am."*

THE SELF-INFLICTED GLASS CEILING

More role reversal is not the answer. The problem here is that we are trying to run two completely incompatible systems. We must choose one or the other.

THE CARER/PROVIDER SYSTEM

The carer/provider system has worked for many thousands of years but is discriminatory to both men and women.

Men trade family life for their career and women trade their career for family life and it is just as much of a problem that men are under represented in family life as it is for women to be under represented in the top jobs.

THE EQUALITY SYSTEM

The equality system is non discriminatory but cannot work in conjunction with a divided carer/provider system. We must stop asking men to pay for everything and stop expecting women to do all the unpaid work.

The age-old argument that men can't or won't do their share of the childcare is questionable.

Most men do want to exercise their human right to a family life, indeed they are screaming it from the rooftops (some of them dressed as batman).

Source:
http://news.bbc.co.uk/2/hi/uk/3652502.stm

Bronnie Ware worked for many years in palliative care. In her book The top five regrets of the dying she has, "*I wish I didn't work so hard*", as number two on her list, she says "*This came from every male patient that I nursed. They missed their children's youth and their partner's companionship.*"

Source:
http://bronnieware.com/regrets-of-the-dying/

There are the women who chose not to work, there are also the single mothers who fight like hell to hold down two low paid jobs and bring up their children but for them the answer is the same, shared parenting and shared providing with both parents doing their fair share of both.

Chapter 19

Is the best man for the job a woman?

EQUALITY FOR WOMEN IS AN OXYMORON

Is the best man for the job a woman?

> *"If money's the god people worship, I'd rather go worship the devil instead."*
>
> Jess C. Scott

If the best man for the job is a woman, give her the job - That's equality.

If the best man for the job is a man, give him the job - That's equality.

If the best man for the job is a man but you give the woman the job anyway - That's discrimination.

If the best man for the job is a woman but you give the man the job anyway - That's discrimination.

QUESTION:

Are women as intelligent as men?

ANSWER:

I personally believe that men and women think in slightly different ways but on balance are equally intelligent.

QUESTION:

Do women have the same strength and stamina as men?

ANSWER:

No of course they don't! It's not even close so if men and women are intellectually equal, what is it that women have that balances men's superior strength and make them equal in the work place?

Example:

I once helped a friend build a garden wall. There was no access to the garden for the lorry delivering the concrete blocks so the driver dropped them at the front door and my friend, his wife and I carried the blocks through the house to the garden.

My friend and I carried two at a time and his wife took one at a time. My friend and I each moved twice as many blocks as his wife. If this were paid work, should the woman have been paid the same as the men?

If I am ever electrocuted and need the kiss of life, the best man for the job is definitely a woman. I want the fire person giving me the kiss of life to be a 'perfect 10' and look just like Kylie Minogue but if I am trapped in a fire on the third floor and need to be carried down a ladder, sorry, Kylie but I want a fire<u>man</u> the bigger and uglier the better!

IS THE BEST MAN FOR THE JOB A WOMAN?

It's illegal, to discriminate between a man and a woman when filling job vacancies but would a builder looking for a hod carrier really choose the woman candidate if she can only lift half the bricks that a man can?

Will the butcher hire a woman who can't carry a side of beef in from the van or the baker take on a woman too feeble to lift a 50kg sack of flour? It's true you can get your flour delivered in 25kg sacks these days but they are more expensive and you make twice as many trips to the flour store when filling the dough mixer.

Sometimes a woman may be the best person for a 'man's job'.

Some jobs that might be best suited to women may include, pilots because in an aircraft more weight equals more fuel so smaller lighter women pilots would be cheaper and better for the environment. Women are also less intimidating when dealing with vulnerable children or adults. The job of white van man may on occasions also be better done by white van woman for example...

Some years ago, while looking for a job I read an advert looking for someone to deliver car parts in a small van. I was surprised to see it was accepted as an exception to the equal opportunities law and only open to women candidates but why?

It seems car mechanics are much more likely to buy car

parts if they are delivered by a pretty young woman than if they are delivered by a big strong man, even if they have to help her unload some of the heavier things from the van. Who would have thought it?

I once had a girlfriend who asked me if I would help her change an engine. I told her car mechanics were not something I was good at and changing an engine was way beyond anything I could do.

"No problem" she said *"I just need you to pass me a few spanners."* We, or more accurately, she changed the engine and not only did the car go afterwards but she didn't have that little pile of bits left over that I always seem to have whenever I work on a car, (perhaps these last two things are connected).

I think she would have made an excellent car-part delivery driver, not only was she young and pretty but she also knew the difference between her o-ring and her circlip and her aquaplane exhaust manifold from her aquaplane cylinder head. That being said the average man has a better knowledge of car parts than the average woman and he is better able to carry them about.

Is it right that the man (in this case me) should have been discriminated against on the grounds of gender?

Alternatively is it right that the company should be legally compelled to take on a male candidate despite them loosing business by that obligation?

If this were solely a commercial decision, men would do all the physical jobs and women would sell the car parts or cars for that matter, draping themselves seductively over the bonnets of the latest sports cars and the like, but I for one do not want to live in a world where profit is the only consideration.

If the point of work were indeed only to make money then the best man for the job may well be a bigger, stronger man who will not leave to have a child but the point of work is not actually to make money.

Work exists only to benefit people! Work is the way we humans as social animals have pooled our resources and assigned the different jobs to those most able to do them to the benefit of all.

Work benefits the employers, the employed and the consumers and should be adapted to give the most benefit to the most people.

If a car mechanic breaks a leg while repairing the doctor's car the doctor will put the leg in plaster. If the doctor tries to fix the car it may never run again and if the mechanic tries fix the leg, the mechanic may never run again.

In this scenario the gender of the doctor and the mechanic are not specified and not relevant. Who does what is decided by training and experience not gender.

When we chose the right person for the job, highly educated women who never fulfill their potential represent a hugely under-utilised resource.

By educating women then making them choose between childcare and a career we are only getting halfway to an equal playing field. The only way to get the full advantage of a universally well-educated population is to share the childcare equally between both parents.

Earlier in this chapter I posed the question *"What do women have that balances a man's superior physical strength?"*

The answer is they do something truly fantastic, amazing and very very necessary. They have babies.

The female body traded the ability to carry heavy loads for the ability to carry a child and together men and women form a partnership that is far far greater than the sum of it's parts and by working as equal partners I believe we can indeed have it all.

Chapter 20

Thinking outside the box

EQUALITY FOR WOMEN IS AN OXYMORON

Thinking outside the box

"Some men look at things the way they are and ask why? I dream of things that are not and ask why not?"

Robert Kennedy

We live in a world of injustice, violence and waste, with pollution threatening to kill us all. We invented money as a tool but it has become our master.

We are all fighting for more money, but ask anyone why, they will tell you it's not to get a bigger slice of the pie but to get their fair share. We are like three year olds, told to help ourselves. There was plenty of pie for all but in the scramble to get our share most of it ended up on the floor or down our clothes.

While working in a supermarket I was told by the store manager my *raison d'être* was to make as much money as possible for the company.

I told him that however hard I worked, my contribution to the company would be an irrelevance to the millionaire company owners, but if the store became inefficient it would be closed which would be a big loss to our customers and an even bigger loss to the employees, so my priorities are to keep the store providing me and my colleagues with employment, to do my part in the process of keeping the town fed and to turn a profit so as to allow the bosses to do their essential part in keeping the whole thing going.

I am not sure this was the answer he was expecting but bosses and workers have bumped along like this for a very long time with workers balancing work and home life and everyone more or less getting what they need but things can no longer go on as they have. Work is changing, life is changing and our expectations are changing all at breakneck speed.

FACT:

Life expectancy is increasing by 3 months per year.

Source:
https://www.nia.nih.gov/research/publication/global-health-and-aging/living-longer

I have even heard a scientist claiming that the first person to live to be 1,000 years old has probably already been born! I can't see him getting away with fifty years of work and nine hundred and thirty years of retirement (I have allowed for twenty years of schooling).

I can do the work of ten men!

I am not super human I just use modern machinery to do the work my grandfather did by hand and it's not just me, all areas of work are now much more efficient.

THINKING OUTSIDE THE BOX

Imagine doing the very thing I'm doing now on a typewriter. You have no spell check, no find and replace, no delete or undo and cut and paste was done with scissors and glue and that's after the invention of the typewriter, before that it was pens and paper and the pens had to be constantly dipped in the ink but the biggest difference of all is the research. Instead of many days of work searching through books in the library I can now find what I want to know at the click of a mouse in less time than it would have taken me to put on my coat.

The most labour intensive part of manufacturing is no longer the making of the object, it's the making of the machine that makes the object but with the rise of 3D printers even this is set to change.

Driverless cars will soon take the place of lorry drivers, bus drivers, taxi drivers etc and they don't need to be 100% safe, just safer than human drivers.

About 35% of current jobs in the UK are at high risk of computerisation over the next 20 years, according to a study by researchers at Oxford University and Deloitte.

Source:
http://www.bbc.com/news/technology-34066941

The idea that we can go on as we have been with a huge workforce, working long hours for low pay is a non-starter.

Since the industrial revolution, jobs have constantly been lost through the advance of technology. The affect of this on employment has been offset by the rise of the consumerism that the industrial revolution also made possible and by the introduction of built-in obsolescence.

Once things were made to last but now there are destructive conflicts of interest in the system. We now build things to break so that we can sell new ones every few years.

The everlasting light bulb bought up and shelved by worried light bulb manufacturers - Fact or urban myth?

The latest computer games won't play on the old games console - Is this just a ploy to sell the new games console?

Built in obsolescence makes good commercial sense but only for the people at the very top who are making all the money.

The workers who are making the product may earn more money because increased sales mean an increase in paid work but they will need to spend the extra money replacing the items they have bought because they too were built to break.

The solution to the build-to-break problem is to print the 'annual cost' on all appropriate items.

The annual cost is the cost of running the item plus the cost of replacing the item, divided by the number of years it will last.

Example.

Two cars that have the same fuel consumption will cost the same to run. If one car lasts twice as long as the other it will also need to be at least twice the price for the annual cost of running and replacing the cars to be the same.

My first energy efficient light bulb came from the Centre for Alternative Technology about 25 years ago. I was told it would last at least 5 years, the first 3 years energy saving would go to offset the high cost of the bulb but the last 2 years would be a genuine money saving.

The price of energy efficient bulbs has dropped considerably but so has how long they last. I am now constantly taking boxes of dead bulbs to be recycled.

The energy needed to source the materials and make the bulbs now out-weighs the energy saving made by the bulbs. My attempt to save money and do my bit for the environment has been sabotaged in the interest of higher profit.

LED bulbs use even less energy and last much much longer. A win win for us and the environment but only until the manufacturers build in a self-destruct component to safeguard their sales.

EQUALITY FOR WOMEN IS AN OXYMORON

A cheap short-life energy efficient bulb will not save the environment and not save me money but if I could see the annual cost next to the energy rating I would see at a glance that the dearer high quality bulb would achieve both my aims with the only losers being the profits of the producers of inferior goods and the wages of those they employ.

I now buy bulbs with a guarantee. Not many people would bother to take back a bulb that only cost a few pounds but I do.

I have a system...

I write the guarantee expiry date on all guaranteed items.

If a bulb fails while under guarantee I can easily see this when I change it but how many of us keep the guarantee for small items and if we did where is it?

I have a system...

I have a ring-binder with a plastic sleeve for every year in which a guarantee ends. I file each new guarantee under the year of expiry.

I now look at the expiry date I wrote on my dud bulb then look in the sleeve for that year and take it back.

At the end of each year all the receipts in the sleeve for the old year will now be out of date so can be recycled and the plastic sleeve put to the back of the folder for reuse.

If we all take things back when they fail too soon, it will become uneconomic for them to keep selling us rubbish.

The commercial conflict of interest in the health industry is even more worrying with the price of life saving drugs determined by what the market will stand.

We still haven't found a cure for the common cold but with treating the symptoms worth billions, why would the drug companies even look?

There have been studies that suggest vitamin D can half your chance of getting a cold or flu but vitamin D is very cheep or free with sunshine so where is the profit?

Source:
http://www.huffingtonpost.com/julie-chen-md/vitamin-d-vs-common-cold-b_6127454.html

There have been studies that suggest tinned or processed tomatoes reduce the risk of prostate cancer but again where is the profit?

Source:
http://jnci.oxfordjournals.org/content/94/5/391.short

It would be unethical to withhold a drug that could cure AIDS, but is it unethical for a drugs company to target their resources in to prolonging the life of AIDS patients who at present have a near normal life expectancy if given their daily cocktail of expensive and profitable drugs.

Can we trust the drug companies to search for the cure that would effectively shoot their golden goose and is it fair to ask them to?

Antibiotics are becoming ineffective. Dame Sally Davies describes this as, *"An antibiotic apocalypse."*

The drug companies know we will need new antibiotic drugs but are reluctant to put in the huge amounts of work and money to produce a drug that they know doctors will hold in reserve and only prescribe when all the old antibiotic drugs have failed in order to extend it's affective years before drug resistance also makes this new drug useless.

The drug companies know that their new drug will probably be out of patent before it goes into unrestricted use so they are unlikely to even get their money back and so very few of them are even looking for the drugs that will save us from Dame Sally's antibiotic apocalypse.

I would like to see drug research done by a non-profit organisation like the NHS with the objective of giving patients the most affective drugs at the cheapest price rather than higher dividends to share holders. Research would then be targeted to where it would do the most good, not to where it would make the most profit. The NHS would look for the drugs that save us the most money while the drug companies

THINKING OUTSIDE THE BOX

look for the drugs that cost us the most!

A drugs research arm of the NHS would have no conflicts of interest so when pricing their drugs they would not need to factor in the billions paid to share holders or the billions paid out every year in fines for dodgy dealing and fraud by the drugs companies.

Source:
http://www.bbc.com/news/business-28212223

If we put 1% our nations wealth (1% of GDP) into a state owned drug research and production company we could sell the drugs to the NHS at cost and to the rest of the world at a reasonable profits, a bit like the way we pay for the BBC to make programs to a high standard, some of which are then sold on to the rest of the world.

We could invite other countries to join us for the sum of 1% of their GDP and pool our resources with all participating countries working together to find the most needed drugs, instead of many drugs companies all working separately on the most potentially profitable drugs and keeping their commercially sensitive findings secret.

This would end the huge conflicts of interest that the private drugs companies have and the money made by one of the most profitable industries in the world would be saved and therefore effectively recycled back into health care.

When money becomes the end instead of the means to an end, we start to make bad decisions based solely on profitability, like the billionaire languishing in jail instead of sipping Champagne on his yacht because despite having more money than he can ever spend he still chooses to get more through tax evasion or the footballer who earns more money than he can spend so he invests it to make even more money.

It's **not** *the economy stupid*, it's the security, health, justice and the happiness of the population that is really important.

If we are to continue to live as we do now, with abundant food, health care, cars to drive and roads to drive them on and all the other things we need or enjoy, then they all need to be produced. This represents the work that needs to be done.

We pay for it all with our earnings but money is not real, it's just a tool we use. As long as the work is getting done we can have all the things we want, money is merely our chosen method of distribution.

Imagine if there were a fire at the Bank of England and £100,000,000,000 went up in smoke, the insurers would not panic. The Lutine Bell would not be rung.

Why?

Because the total cost to the insurer is just £200,000, they would only payout £100,000 for the warehouse and £100,000 for the paper. Money is just paper, a credit note for work done.

Forget "*I need to earn enough money to buy the things I need*", instead think "*We must produce the things we need and we can use money as a tool to help us do so.*"

If we could all work like ants everyone working tirelessly for the common good and taking only what we need, there would be no need for money at all. Unfortunately humans are not like ants and without money we would all tend to spend our time collecting more of the available pie for ourselves rather than increasing the size of the pie.

The capitalist system we use has helped us produce great wealth in the west. Our standard of living is beyond the wildest dreams of even our grandparents.

Malnutrition is almost only ever due to eating the wrong food or mental illness rather than any lack of available food. We all have, TVs, smart phones, GPS, computers all considered normal to even the poorest in the UK. The average value of house contents is around £40,000 and on one weekend alone 1.5 million of us flew off from just one airport.

Source:
http://www.telegraph.co.uk/finance/personalfinance/insurance/buildingsandcontent/8260054/6.8-million-homes-are-underinsured.html

We really are doing OK but it all comes at a price. Busy stressful lives working long hours and the energy and resources we consume are an environmental disaster. Long term this is not sustainable and sooner rather than later things are going to have to change.

There are two possible outcomes:

We reduce dramatically the world population, reduce dramatically the amount each of us consume, share the world's resources more fairly and live our lives with far fewer possessions.

In this scenario we would each have less personal wealth but more time to enjoy the things we do have.

Option two...

The global population continues to increase, climate change will flood large amounts of farmland and turn other parts into desert, reducing our ability to produce food for an ever-increasing population. The lack of food will lead to famine, social breakdown and wars over land and water, which will reduce the population until we reach a sustainable level.

To avoid this we need to consume less and work less both of which are doable with huge advantages and very little cost to us.

How to consume less...

At least 90% of the things in your house you don't need and 50% you probably don't even want. The problem is government can never encourage us to consume less because that would lead to a drop in demand and the dreaded economic recession or even a depression making us all poorer, but if you don't want half the things you have now, then you can get a lot poorer before anything bad happens at all!

FACT:

A third of all the food we buy is never eaten (1.3 Billion tons a year).

Source:
https://dairygood.org/content/2016/produced-but-never-eaten-food-waste-solutions

This is bad management on our part. Here is a simple tip - Shop for food after you have eaten. If you are hungry, you buy 25% more food that's why supermarkets are filled with the smell of roasting chickens and why the hot bread smell from the bakery extractor fan is directed back into the store.

Because the food goes in your trolley and not into your stomach you stay hungry and so you buy much more than you need or want with the extra going into landfill at great cost to you and the environment.

How many shoes do you have? And how many feet?

Thought so!

Of course you need different shoes for different seasons and your wellies won't look right with that little black dress but some surveys suggest one in ten women spend more than £1,000 a year on shoes while 8% own more than 100 pairs each and seven out of ten women admitted having shoes they had never worn. Men are not immune to this, just in a slightly different league.

If we spent less time working we would have less money to buy shoes but more time to wear the ones we already have.

LESS CAN BE MORE

A little while ago I had a massive cull of small cute furry animals, the ones of the soft toy variety that is.

It became clear to me that my childrens' lives were being blighted by 'stuff'.

The house rule is that there is no TV at the weekend until your bedroom is tidy, well at least to a point where you can see enough floor to warrant bringing up the vacuum. This lead to a battle every weekend, with my 8 and 10 year old children spending most of the weekend in a half-hearted attempt to clear the mountain of clothes and toys.

I decided to make some changes. I told them they could have five furry animal toys each and filled two and a half

THINKING OUTSIDE THE BOX

bin bags with the rest and put them in the loft.

Next the books - They were allowed ten each and the rest went into a locked cupboard (locking away books! How bad a parent am I?) It's not quite that bad, it operates like a library you change your books whenever you want to, provided you can find a parent with the key who is not too busy.

On to clothes. If you can live out of a suit case for two weeks on holiday you shouldn't need that much more when you have full access to a washing machine, so we sorted all the clothes into piles - Trousers here, jumpers there and clothes that were too big or not suitable for this time of year went into an enormous box to be gone through when the season changes and summer clothes will once again be needed.

We then went through the clothes, pile-by-pile hanging up the clothes we needed and a few spares, choosing only the best of the bunch to keep and carefully leaving out the impractical things like those white trousers that look good on, but only for about an hour before they are ready for the wash again and anything that needs to be ironed, washed separately or god forbid, hand washed!

The rest about half went to the charity shop. I should just point out here that most of their clothes were passed on so out of their twelve coats, I didn't actually buy any.

There was one other thing I needed to do - *"The emergency*

hanger." The emergency hanger is a full set of clothes, ready for instant use. This set stays on the rail only to be used if there are no other clothes left and it's time for school or the like but if you need the emergency hanger this means you haven't been putting your clothes in the wash, so you loose a point on the points chart which has an adverse affect on pocket money.

So far, so good. On to the toys…

Professor Pat Pending's 2nd law of distribution states that… *"All toys that are in lots of parts such as jigsaws and Lego, will become evenly distributed around the room."*

These toys are not played with from one year to the next because of the time and effort needed to amass the pieces. These and all the other toys were collected and put into their boxes, crates or ice-cream tubs then into the locked cupboard on the same system as the books. Anything broken went in the bin and anything outgrown went into the loft. (It's hard to get rid of once loved toys).

This all took a long time but the net result is that well over three quarters of the 'stuff' that was in the rooms has now been removed and the children haven't missed any of it.

The clothes are more available - Yes with fewer clothes, more are available because the clothes you want aren't buried under a mountain of things you don't want. Toys are played with until they become boring then changed for some not seen for ages and never again is Lego stood on with bare feet first thing in the morning and the tidying up no longer takes the whole weekend.

My point is that less really can be more and our advertising fueled obsession with buying more and more is actually having an adverse affect on our quality of life.

The same process can be used to declutter the rest of the house but if our goal is to reduce the environmental cost and the unnecessary work involved in producing unwanted goods, then the answer is to simply not buy them in the first place.

Children constantly change their size and their interests and require a constantly changing supply of clothes and toys. From baby grows to school uniforms, from rattles to computer games. As adults we still change but at a more sedate pace. We may not use the tennis racket as often as we used to but we can at least kid ourselves we will take it up again one day and when we do, we might even get back into the clothes we have grown out of.

This means fewer of our clothes and possessions are hand-me-downs, so we get to choose what we buy and we buy only what we want or at least what we think we want. This ought to work well, everyone buys what they want and leaves the rest, zero waste. Brilliant!

So what goes wrong?

Three of the biggest problems are fashion, built in obsolescence, deliberate short product life and Christmas.

Fashion is nothing more than someone else telling you what to wear and then charging you ten times the price to do so and a fashion victim is a person that gives in to this extortion.

There is no increase in quality in fashion clothes, they won't last any longer. Fashion is just built in obsolescence.

In one year, clothes that were your pride and joy become unwearable through nothing more than dictated opinion. Our wardrobes are full of clothes that are just too passé.

Without fashion we can still chose clothes that suit us. We can still chose clothes that accentuate or hide our lumps and bumps depending on whether or not they are supposed to be there. The only bit of the fashion industry that needs to change is the bit that makes it time sensitive.

The music on my phone includes modern day and classical music spanning hundreds of years yet if I were to walk the streets in my kaftan, flairs and platform shoes I'd be the subject of ridicule.

I have this recurring dream in which all the top designers are sitting round a table eating caviar and drinking Champagne. They are all laughing at us and saying that we would buy whatever they chose to sell us and at whatever price they cared to ask as long as it has a designer name on it. Then one of them gets up and says, "*I can make the mugs buy any name I want.*" Then someone else shouts out "*Go on then, make 'Joe Bloggs' into a designer name, if you're so good*" and the rest is history.

The end of December sees Christmas, supposedly a religious festival but the most often heard prayer is "*Oh my God what can I get this year for...*"

We run around spending money we can't afford, desperately trying to find things for people who want for nothing and end up giving them something they would have already bought for themselves had they actually wanted it. So they end up with something else to go into their already groaning loft.

The longest queues in December are actually after Christmas when we take the things back that we would much rather not have been given in the first place, but what about the fun, the magic, peace on earth, good will to all men, children sitting on Santa's knee, the carols, the most wonderful time of the year and all that?

The sad truth is, the myth and reality are poles apart.

For a lot of people, Boxing Day morning means waking up thinking "*Thank God that's all over for another year*" or "*I so need a holiday.*" For many it's time to start paying back the overspend, but the New Year also sees a massive spike in people filing for divorce and not just divorce, there is a massive rise in domestic violence, robbery, theft, adultery and drink driving.

The most wonderful time of the year is filled with gluttony, drunkenness and sexual promiscuity. The whole thing is driven not by love or the desire to give pleasure to friends and family, or even religion, (after all it's a mostly a Pagan festival, which is why we celebrate at the solstices and why we bring evergreen trees into the house such as holly, ivy and of course the Christmas tree).

Christmas is fueled by commercialism and emotional blackmail. We buy for them because they buy for us and once you are in the cycle there is no way out. You may not speak to someone from one year to the next, but still feel obliged to trudge round the heaving shops looking for inspiration as to what you could give them. Your only motivation is to get another name ticked off the list.

The best present you could give this year is a "Christmas-Free card" - Yes they do exist! A company called Charmed Zone does actually sell them on Amazon. You send your friends and family a card announcing that this year you are not entering into the ecological disaster that is Christmas and no cards or presents will be sent or accepted. With the exception of e-cards perhaps.

Source:
https://www.amazon.co.uk/dp/B01MYM29K1

THINKING OUTSIDE THE BOX

If we stop buying things we don't want this will lead to many thousands of job losses, or we could all just work a bit less and give the people we care about some of the time we have saved by not working and not shopping quite so much.

There are some important jobs, necessary for our survival such as food production and medicine. I also count bringing a child into the world, educating and caring for that child in this group.

In our society medicine is relatively well paid, but food production is mostly done at or around minimum wage and much of the work of bringing up our children is not normally paid at all.

Jobs that are not necessary for survival such as entertainment, sport or art, are often valued far more highly with the likes of Jonathan Ross and Fabio Capello being paid £6,000,000 a year and Wayne Rooney is reputedly on an amazing £35,000,000. That's £673,000 a week for playing football, which equates to more money in a week than a food worker on minimum wage earns in her entire working life!

Is a footballer really worth that much more than the men and women who put food on our tables?

If our society were to breakdown due to shortages of food and water caused by climate change, with gangs roaming the streets then in a world where the only rule was survival of the strongest, *Pickled Cows* and *Unmade Beds* would be nothing more than something to eat and somewhere to sleep. Of course art and entertainment have value but I think we have the balance a bit wrong.

A man who buys and sells things that don't exist with money he hasn't got in the city will get an annual bonus worth more than the lifetimes earnings of a lollypop man who risks his own life to protect our children from serious injury or death.

The Utopian world we were promised in the seventies where machines do the work and we all spend our endless leisure time doing interesting things is still possible, but not until we free ourselves from the fallacy that work is good and more work is better and realise that money is not an end in itself, merely a means to an end.

Sustainability can be achieved by reducing the global population to no more than 50% of the present levels and building things to last instead of building things to break therefore using the world's resources more efficiently.

By sharing the pie more fairly there would be enough for all. The real injustices is not the 10% difference between the earnings of men and women but the £15,000 to £5,000,000 difference between the earnings of those at the top (mostly men) and those on low earnings.

I have read that after £40,000 a year, more money doesn't

make you any happier so why go on earning? Why become one of Bronnie Ware's regretters, looking back on a life spent working to accumulate money you didn't need?

Equality can be achieved but only when we break the carer/provider divide and treat discrimination as a problem for both sexes.

One sex is not universally oppressing the other. We are all the victims and also the beneficiaries of discrimination.

Sustainability can be achieved but not until sustainability rather than profit becomes our goal.

The amount of work that needs to be done is finite. If people work longer into their lives there will be more workers so not enough work for us all to continue working at the same rate. We need to share the work that does need to be done more fairly.

It's shear madness to have a man working 80 hours a week while his neighbour is out of work and living on benefits.

When George Osbourne was chancellor of the exchequer, he said he wanted to help the owner of the corner shop who stayed open until midnight to support their family and the commuter who leaves home before the children are up and comes back long after they have gone to bed, because they want a better life for their children but an absent parent, regardless of whether it's due to divorce or excessive work is rarely the best thing for a child.

We are tied to a system of money that has served us well in the past but is becoming less and less fit for purpose. The present system has become unsustainable and will continue to get more so, until we do something about it.

The way to restore sustainability is to work less per week or per year but to go on much longer in life. As a result we would all be able to enjoy more free time while we are younger. The work/life balance would become much easier. Life would be much richer. Gone would be the days of seventy or eighty hour weeks where you spend your whole life in the cycle of: Work, eat, sleep, repeat.

It all sounds great but how can we afford to live on part time wages? I believe there is a way and the advantages include…

> Break the carer/provider gender divide;
>
> End child poverty;
>
> Reduce child abuse;
>
> Achieve childcare parity;
>
> Achieve gender parity with child contact;
>
> Reduce the number of divorces;
>
> Massively reduce our carbon footprint;
>
> Massively reduce our use of the world's finite resources;

THINKING OUTSIDE THE BOX

Achieve gender pay parity (at all ages);

Increase productivity;

Increase the availability of highly trained and skilled workers;

Get the work we need to do done and have far more leisure time;

Make work pay;

Massively reduce the benefits bill;

Achieve gender parity in career achievement;

Boost the economy;

Make our country a much, much, much fairer place!

I believe this is all possible, we just need to think outside the box. Quite a long way outside the box.

How do we achieve all this?

Simple we all do a thirty hour week and children pay for their own childhood.

If we all do a 30 hour week we can still get the job done and still have enough time to do our share of the childcare.

With childcare divided equally between both parents, women would no longer need to stop working for years or rely on their husbands for money. It would become an equal partnership with women no more likely to accept low paid work than men, affectively removing one of the main causes of wage discrimination but is it possible?

The average amount of work done by each worker in the UK is just over 32 hours a week so it's not a very big change in the average but a massive shift in distribution of the work and the small shortfall will easily be made up by the thousands of women who will no longer need to abandon their careers to look-after their children.

Source:
https://stats.oecd.org/Index.aspx?DataSetCode=ANHRS

Employers already know that making work childcare friendly, gives them access to a workforce of millions of women. If making work childcare friendly gave them access to all workers with children, they would soon change the working hours to the parents and their own advantage.

The new working hours may look more like three days of ten hours with mothers and fathers working on different days or Mum working 5 morning shifts of 6 hours and Dad doing the same in the afternoon.

Take away the need for career breaks and mothers will finally have a level playing field in the work place and fathers will get to do more of the caring, so win-win.

Going on as we have is not an option. It is inevitable that we will soon have to stop asking who pays for whom and expect everyone (as far as is possible) to pay for themselves.

Imagine if you can, a world where children were expected to pay for their own care, accruing debts, something like a student loan to be paid back during their years of work.

If children paid for themselves and mothers continued to work then fathers would no longer be expected to earn for the whole family. We cannot expect men to pay for themselves, their wives and their children yet not earn the extra money needed to do so.

This would remove the compulsion for men to chose only high paid work that will bring in enough money to pay for the whole family and with shared childcare women will no longer be compelled to chose only the low paid jobs that fit in with the children.

The tax breaks and benefits paid to parents would become unnecessary as would be the billions spent on deciding and enforcing child maintenance.

All children would be taken out of poverty at a stroke. Too many children by accident of birth have no realistic chance of achieving very much in their lives, this is a tragic waste!

The cost of this would be enormous and children would reach maturity with huge debts because each child would pay for their own upbringing, but the costs would be distributed equally between everyone and the unfair benefits enjoyed by the childless who nether pay for their own upbringing or that of their children would be ended.

The cost of bringing up a child is already paid for in one form or another so this would be less expensive over all as we would save the cost of taking tax with one hand and giving it back to parents in the form of benefits with the other.

At the other end of life we must also put money by for our own old age. We can buy insurance against the cost of a care home should it be needed and we can decide for ourselves whether to use the value of our house to offset the costs of our old age or put-by more and give the house to our children.

There will always be some who will never be able to provide for themselves and we will have to share the cost of these people but most of us will be able to live self-sufficient lives without the need for benefits. We would have a much better work/home-life balance and instead of the young, the middle aged and often the old having all the disposable income it would be more evenly distributed throughout our lives eliminating the financial bottleneck of the childcare years.

It's time to once again make money our slave not our master and in the battle of the sexes it's time to call a truce and fight the real enemies of discrimination, men and women together as equalists.

THINKING OUTSIDE THE BOX

If you agree with the views in this book, do something about it. Help raise awareness, ring radio shows, write to The Times, stand on your soapbox on Speaker's Corner, lend this book to someone (although thinking about my royalties you better buy them a copy for Christmas, or not!)

The one thing we must not do is nothing. If we do nothing we will stumble along until the inevitable consequences of our inaction will force our hand by which time, the problems and the solutions will be a good deal harder.

EQUALITY FOR WOMEN IS AN OXYMORON

Appendix

Helplines and useful contacts

EQUALITY FOR WOMEN IS AN OXYMORON

Helplines and useful contacts

Correct at time of publication, however some changes will occur over time

If you are in immediate danger call 999

GENERAL SUPPORT

Samaritans:
Tel UK: 116 123
Tel ROI: 1850 60 90 90
Email: jo@samaritans.org
Website: https://www.samaritans.org/

Rape Crisis:
Tel: 0808 802 9999
Website: http://www.rapecrisis.org.uk

Shelter:
Tel: 0344 515 2000
Website: http://www.shelter.org.uk

Victim support:
Tel: 0808 168 9111
Website: http://www.victimsupport.org.uk

Crimestoppers:
Tel: 0800 555 111
Website: http://www.crimestoppers-uk.org

HELP FOR FATHER'S

The Fathers for Justice:
Website: http://www.fathers-4-justice.org/

Dads UK Forum:
Website: http://www.separateddads.co.uk

Families Need Fathers
Helpline: 0300 0300 363
(Mon - Fri 9am - 10pm & weekends 10am - 3pm)
Email: fnf@fnf.org.uk
Website: http://www.fnf.org.uk
Facebook: https://www.facebook.com/Families-Need-Fathers-231208770254871/

HELPLINES AND USEFUL CONTACTS

HELP FOR MALE VICTIMS OF DOMESTIC VIOLENCE

Men's Aid:
Abduction, child abuse, domestic violence, family law, family law reform, false allegations, human rights, sex discrimination.
Helpline: 0333 567 0556 (Mon - Sat 11am - 9pm)
Email: help@MensAid.co.uk
Website: http://www.mensaid.co.uk

AMEN (Ireland):
Helpline and support service for male victims of domestic violence and their children.
Helpline: 046 9023 718
Email: info@amen.ie
Website: http://www.amen.ie

The Dyn Project (area served Wales):
Helpline providing support to all men who are experiencing domestic abuse in Wales.
Helpline: 0808 801 0321

Fylde Coast Men's Support Association, formerly MRSA (Lancashire):
Help and support to male victims of rape, adult male survivors of childhood sexual abuse and male victims of domestic/partner violence.
Tel: 07932 898274
Email: malerapemrsa@yahoo.co.uk

HELP FOR FEMALE VICTIMS OF DOMESTIC VIOLENCE

Women's Aid refuge:
Run in partnership between Women's Aid and Refuge.
Tel: 0808 200 0247 (24 hour)
Email: helpline@womensaid.org.uk
Website: http://www.nationaldomesticviolencehelpline.org.uk

Northern Ireland Women's Aid:
Helpline: 0808 8021414
Tel: 028 90 249041
Email: info@womensaidni.org
Website: http://www.niwaf.org

Scottish Women's Aid:
Helpline: 0800 2000247
Tel: 0131 226 6606
Email: contact@scottishwomensaid.org.uk

Welsh Women's Aid:
Helpline: 0800 2000247

HELPLINES AND USEFUL CONTACTS

SUPPORT FOR DOMESTIC VIOLENCE AND LINKS FOR LEGAL ADVICE

ManKind Initiative:
Helpline: 01823 334244 (10am to 4pm)
Website: http://www.mankind.org.uk

SAM - Systematic Abuse of Males:
Website: http://www.samonline.org.uk

RELATIONSHIP, FAMILY AND SEX COUNSELLING

Relate:
Tel: 0300 100 1234
Website: http://www.relate.org.uk
Facebook: http://www.facebook.com/pages/Relate-the-relationship-people/125872990762163?ref=ts

HELP FOR GRANDPARENTS

Grandparents Apart UK:
Self-help group for Grandparents.
Tel: Margaret: 0141 882 5658
June: 01560 322937
Email: grandparentskk@btinternet.com
Website: http://grandparentsapart.co.uk/

HELP FOR PERPETRATORS

Respect:
Helpline: 0808 802 4040 (Mon - Fri 9am - 5pm)
Tel: 020 7022 1801
Email: info@respectphoneline.org.uk
Website : http://respectphoneline.org.uk/

Men's Advice:
Helpline: 0808 801 0327 (Mon - Fri 9am - 5pm)
Email: info@mensadviceline.org.uk
Website: http://www.mensadviceline.org.uk

Support line:
Helpline: 01708 765200 *(hours vary so ring for details)*
Email: info@supportline.org.uk
Website: http://www.supportline.org.uk/problems/anger_management.php

British Association of Anger Management (London):
Tel: 0345 1300 286 (Mon - Fri 9am - 5pm)
Email: info@angermanage.co.uk
Website: www.angermanage.co.uk

LAST BUT NOT LEAST

Contact James Judd:
Questions and comments can be addressed to:
Twitter: https://twitter.com/judd_author